Conscious Femininity

Marie-Louise von Franz, Honorary Patron

**Studies in Jungian Psychology
by Jungian Analysts**

Daryl Sharp, General Editor

Conscious Femininity

Interviews with
MARION WOODMAN

Introduction and Two Articles
by Marion Woodman

To men and women who are struggling to know themselves
in order to know each other.

Canadian Cataloguing in Publication Data

Woodman, Marion
    Conscious femininity: interviews with Marion Woodman

(Studies in Jungian psychology by Jungian analysts; 58)

Includes bibliographical references and index.

ISBN 0-919123-59-7

1. Woodman, Marion—Interviews. 2. Femininity (Psychology).
3. Women (Psychology). 4. Psychoanalysts—Canada—Interviews.
5. Women psychoanalysts—Canada—Interviews.
I. Title.   II. Series.

HQ1206.W664 1993   155.6'33   C92-095115-5

INNER CITY BOOKS
Box 1271, Station Q, Toronto, Canada M4T 2P4
Telephone (416) 927-0355
FAX 416-924-1814

Honorary Patron: Marie-Louise von Franz.
Publisher and General Editor: Daryl Sharp.
Senior Editor: Victoria Cowan.

INNER CITY BOOKS was founded in 1980 to promote the
understanding and practical application of the work of C.G. Jung.

Cover photo by Bryn Douglass.

Index by Daryl Sharp

Printed and bound in Canada by John Deyell Company

Contents

6 Contents

Two Papers by Marion Woodman:

See final page for descriptions of other Inner City Books

Introduction

Proofreading these interviews has sent alarming shivers into my solar plexus. I imagine I am standing at the center of fifteen surrounding mirrors. I look into one. I turn. I am looking back at myself from a different angle. Some angles I like better than others; some I prefer not to see. I have to keep breathing into my belly to test the validity of the image in the mirror.

I am astonished at some of the statements I made six years ago. They now seem so straightforward, so definitive. Experience has taught me the subtleties inherent in their simplicity, teasing me into deeper questions and fewer answers. Fortunately I never cease to ask questions and, while several themes recur in these intertwining discussions, each time they return they resonate with new overtones and new undertones. The woman who speaks "In Her Own Voice" in 1992 has lived in rooms in her psyche unknown to the woman interviewed for *The Tarrytown Letter* in 1985. But while my psychic home has expanded up, down, back and through, its core has not changed.

I am still asking, "What is conscious femininity?" Like all the questions in my life, I cannot know the meaning of the question until I have found the answer. I cannot know Sophia, the feminine nature of God, until I have experienced her love radiating in my cells. I cannot experience that radiation until I love the reality of my cells, a reality that is constantly renewing itself in their death and rebirth. Nor can I love the reality of my cells until I have known them, felt their anguish, heard their purring, seen them with my fingers, ears and eyes. And perceived their dying and reviving dance in the fire of my imagination. Whatever is not essence is being burned away. The question still remains. Each time I try to answer it, I answer from where I am. One thing I do know. The answer asks the question. So long as I keep asking the question, I know the answer is there, struggling to speak in a way that I can finally comprehend.

Another thing I know is that the written word cannot capture the totality-in-flux of the conscious feminine. My mind struggles to organize the exact words that will clarify my thoughts, as if it could reduce their motion to stillness. My heart strives to contain the Dionysian joy that sometimes threatens to overwhelm my prose. Meantime, my body watches quietly, taking the theorizing with a grain of Sophia's salt. She knows her time will come. Her curly-headed clown will spontaneously explode into slapstick or play. She loves play, reveling in whatever strikes her imagination in the moment. Sometimes she is a sultry gypsy. She can stride into conventional society and, just by being who she is, turn things upside down. In seeing the whole of things, the so-called light and dark, she absorbs both.

I remember one time pondering Sophia's depths as I changed from workshop pants to lecture dress in the dark vestry of a Malibu church. Suddenly, I was caught naked in the glare of a custodian's light. Simultaneously, I saw myself both pontificating in the pulpit upstairs and bare as a poor, forked animal below. My belly convulsed in Buddha laughter. The imagery of mind and heart were *realized* in the unity of my body's response.

To feminine consciousness, the spiritual and the physical are two aspects of one totality. Spirit confirms body, articulates body's wisdom. Spirit is immediate and actual, not something arrived at, as in Plato, through dialectical ascent. "As above, so below" translates into "as in the head, so in the belly"; the two are simultaneously present, not dialogically opposed. The paradox of this simultaneous presence—the solar plexus in the head and the head in the solar plexus—resists the logic of prose, demanding poetry's elliptical leaps which metaphor attempts to encompass. In my introduction to *The Pregnant Virgin,* I called this paradox "frog conjunctions," thinking of frogs among lilypads leaping from leaf to leaf.

Metaphor is the language of the soul. Through a physical image, metaphor reveals a spiritual truth or condition. Take, for example, a line from a Zen koan: "Hide yourself in the middle of the flames." We see the picture and, if we understand metaphor at all, we don't smirk and say, "Who'd be dumb enough to hide in a fire?" Rather we understand we're being challenged to risk all in our passion for life, and our cells shout *yes.* Just as metaphor encompasses spirit and body, so, as I use the term, soul is the meeting place of spirit and body, the eternal part of us that lives in body while we are on Earth. Soul is traditionally feminine in both men and women.

At the lectern, as anywhere else—even here at my desk, witnessing a spiritual and physical event as the sun rises at 6:43—I cannot repeatedly articulate the inherent paradox of spirit as body in every image. Unless, perhaps, like Eve in the Garden before the Fall, I might choose to deliver my lectures in the condition in which that custodian surprised me. The feminine, however disguised, is always naked, in the sense of "seeing through" in order to reveal. Apocalypse means unveiling.

In rereading these interviews, I realize that at times I was too optimistic. I put too much hope in outer events like the fall of the Berlin Wall, the dissolution of the U.S.S.R., the rebellion against patriarchal dictatorship in Eastern Europe. I underestimated the blind tenacity with which, at any cost, patriarchy holds on to its obsolete power. Stalin was prepared to purge even to extinction. Hitler was ready to destroy the globe rather than see it wrested from his rule. What began as a neurotic drive for power, when threatened by defeat, turned into psychosis. We see evidence of this behavior in the world today in civil and international wars. We also see it in individuals.

Patriarchs, men and women who have no concept of conscious femininity, are locked in an energy that blinds their eyes and deafens their ears to their own unconscious rage. They believe they have feminine feeling, but their blind devotion to Great Mother in whatever form—state, church, corporation, university—has cut off their connection to their own soul values. This lack of soul connection results in unconscious projections that can be diabolic in their intensity. Anger quickly seethes into rage, distrust into contempt. Individuals whose egos are battered and bewildered by the chaos of collapsing structures can quickly succumb to possession by unconscious forces. While I still have faith in divine purpose, I am increasingly sobered by the depths of unconsciousness to be overcome and the kind of inner strength necessary to prevail. Is it not inconceivable that in 1992 we tenaciously hold on to an order of society that is in reality enacting its own extinction?

As I read through these interviews, I hear some of my readers saying, "Why waste my time with dreams when I may lose my job? Why indulge myself reading about soul when I'm losing my marriage? Why bother with dead ideas when I can barely pay my mortgage?"

The point is that the loss of soul connection, loss of connection to our femininity, may be the real cause of our anguished condition. If we have no bridge to the unconscious depths that drive us, our rational attempts to correct our situation are merely Band-Aids. They work only so long as we remain cut off from the living fire inside. When that fire blazes forth, our Band-Aids go up in smoke.

Without reflection on our inner world, we succumb to broad generalizations. Then patriarchy is confused with masculinity; femininity is defended with those same patriarchal power tools it so fiercely derides; fitness is confused with body awareness, with no attempt to listen to body messages. Generalizations petrify into fixations which cannot change so long as we ourselves are fixed on refusing to see, sleepwalking through life. We sleepwalk when we fail to listen to our soul's yearning, fail to name a lie, fail to recognize the passion that smolders in our inner volcanoes.

In *The Tibetan Book of the Dead,* those who enter the Bardo must first be persuaded they are dead. T.S. Eliot in *The Waste Land* (1922) reflects a hollow society living in a desert without water. Samuel Beckett in *Endgame* (1958) creates an eight-by-eight kingdom ruled by a blind patriarch who bullies his dependent slave, although both know they are dependent on each other for survival. It is a deadlock situation. The only hope of redemption in each case lies in the consciousness that can see the condition. Without that objective observer, and the desire to connect with the inner dynamics, there can be neither conscious femininity nor conscious masculinity. There is simply no way to bridge inner and outer.

More than once in these interviews I refer to the Vietnam War Memorial designed by Maya Lin, which in the short period of ten years since its dedication has become one of the most revered icons in America. It is ceaselessly touched by human fingers stroking letter by letter the 58,183 names enshrined on it. (I think of Russian icons of Sophia which, in an earlier age, received the same love.) Human hands touching the black reflecting granite, fingers tracing letter by letter a beloved name—here is the Word become flesh. Here too is nature becoming conscious matter or the conscious feminine. The embodiment of that consciousness is for me nowhere more poignantly enacted than in a human hand caressing a beloved name, resurrecting into a new life, a new consciousness, what was sacrificed in an old order. We have never inhabited this space before.

Commenting on a mandala whose center was left empty, Jung said that its center was in the new era, the era which we have now entered. We are the observing center of the mandala which now revolves within human consciousness as consciousness expands to encompass the globe. The globe is a mandala whose center is us, whose center is the consciousness we bring to it. Our consciousness is the perceiver that can change the perceived.

Needless to say, the "us" at the center of the global mandala is not the unredeemed patriarchal ego which has ruled the planet since its human discovery as a globe. The us who will one day live in the center of that mandala will be both masculine and feminine, united in a partnership of equals. That union transcends without denying gender; gender is the differentiated manifestation of the oneness that transcends it. To call the us at the center "androgynous," with its primitive associations, is inadequate to what we as conscious beings and world citizens are becoming. Perhaps a better understanding lies in the concept of human identity coming into consciousness through recognition of what is foreign to us, not as alien, but as the instrument of recognition. The feminine is the instrument of recognition of the masculine, as the masculine is the instrument of recognition of the feminine. The one is present in the other as the instrument of consciousness itself.

Toward the emergence of that consciousness in both men and women, these interviews are addressed. God and Goddess, forever being discovered through the work of individuals, unite us all in a global community we are only now beginning to discover.

Marion Woodman
Toronto

Acknowledgments

All due effort was made to obtain permission from copyright holders for the interviews and articles used in this book. Marion Woodman and Inner City Books are grateful for permissions granted.

Original sources and interviewers are indicated in footnotes. Due to editorial considerations the interviews may not appear here exactly as originally published.

1

Anorexia, Bulimia and Addiction*

Artist Martha Graham once said, "The body does not lie." America's fore-most dancer/choreographer, after more than ninety years of movement, knows about the rich expressions of the body. But so should we. In fact, the harder we look at our aches and ailments, the more we will be startled by the painful truths they are trying to convey.

For the last six years Toronto analyst Marion Woodman has been ex-ploring some of the most intractable of our modern illnesses, from alco-holism to anorexia. Recently she told Tarrytown what these ravaging dis-eases are saying about our dangerously disembodied way of life.

Tarrytown: Why are we seeing such an astonishing increase in eating disorders today?

Woodman: Anorexia and bulimia are more common because women are further away from their bodies than ever. This breeds a profound inner rage, one that compounds itself from generation to generation.

Yet I believe illnesses like anorexia, far from being evil, are the means of healing on a larger scale if we can only understand their message.

Food represents nurturing by the mother, and when we reject it, like the anorexic, we are rejecting life itself. Women today are being forced to deal with their own death wish, which is precisely what we must do on a global scale. The truth is we are moving toward annihilation because our culture does not respect the earth or feminine creativity.

Young anorexic women are actually more fortunate than the obese, be-cause they confront their wish to die. The obese can play around with the body's warnings usually until menopause. Then they are trapped in an ar-mored body and stuck with the despair of an unlived life.

Tarrytown: How is our rejection of the body related to our rejection of the feminine?

Woodman: All matter is feminine. On this level, men's bodies are em-bodiments of the feminine just as much as women's. The extraordinary

* Reprinted from *The Tarrytown Letter,* no. 54 (Dec. 1985/Jan. 1986). The interview was conducted by contributing editor Sally Van Wagenen Keil.

13

thing is that matter is becoming conscious. For women, there is an anguished realization: "I hate this body!" For men, it comes out in the cry, "It hurts!"

Matter is forcing many people to become aware of its sacredness. So we have these scourges of illness like messages from the gods.

Tarrytown: What can we learn from eating disorders?

Woodman: Anorexia and bulimia tell us that our souls are starving. Also that our lives have become too heady. These people are cut off at the neck. They have lived life as a performance. There is no ego center in the body, no "I" who senses and feels in the gut. And so they complain they have no *experience* of their lives.

People who are addicted to food—or even to alcohol and drugs—are terrified of the body and of reality. Their whole life may be a mask which they use to deal with the outside world. Instead of reacting from their own feeling values, their first response is "How can I please in this situation?"

They are also addicted to control and to perfectionism. They try to be so efficient every day, then they go home and all hell breaks loose in binging, partying, drinking or some demonic ritual. This addiction to perfection is a major problem of our culture.

Tarrytown: How does this addiction play itself out?

Woodman: If you think you have to be the perfect son or daughter, you will drive yourself relentlessly to achieve. This actually is a desire for death not life. It means making life into a perfect and lifeless structure.

Will power can keep such people going for a long time, if they can keep running fast enough and the body is strong enough—but finally the body will collapse through fatigue because the power principle kills life.

Tarrytown: When do people come to you for help?

Woodman: Usually not until they are desperate and finally have to listen to their illness. Until then, the body seemingly lives its own independent life. When the body becomes ill they feel victimized by its symptoms.

The truth is they are starving for an inner life. In fact, eating disorders often have very little to do with the number of calories taken in. Many fat women, for example, actually eat less than thin women. The problem may be that the blocked energy goes into fat. In therapy, we try to find out why.

Tarrytown: What generally is blocking life?

Woodman: A profound unconscious fear and rage that goes back to infancy. Because our mothers could not love themselves as complete feminine beings, they could not love us as feminine beings. So our fear is archetypal, monstrous.

We have a tremendous sense of something within being shut off, abandoned. This is our own self, our own soul.

Tarrytown: So our bodies are like abandoned children?

Woodman: Exactly. This abandonment may even go back before birth to time spent in the uterus. One often finds that children whom the mother attempted to abort are traumatized by the fear that they are going to be annihilated.

But this abortion can also be figurative. A parent can "love" a child, but the love may be conditional.

A mother who is trying to mold a child into a work of art cannot accept the instinctual side of the child—the living organic "puking and peeing" side—because she cannot accept her own body. So the child is separated from its body as well.

Tarrytown: How do people deal with this rejection?

Woodman: Food symbolizes Mother. The bulimic wants Mother so desperately she just gorges her down. But the minute she's in her stomach, she can't assimilate her, so she vomits. The anorexic refuses and rejects Mother until she wastes away from her lack of inner nourishment.

The body is like an elaborate metaphor. One may be able to taste and not swallow, like the anorexic, or to swallow and not integrate like the bulimic or the obese.

Tarrytown: How do you proceed from here?

Woodman: You have to get at the meaning of the starvation—what the soul is hungry for—in order to feed it.

An addict attempts to fill a terrible emptiness inside. But it's spiritual emptiness, not physical emptiness.

Dreams give us images that can feed the soul. I really think that the body probably manifests in every dream, if you can read it physically as well as psychologically. If a person dreams that part of their house is on fire, that may mean there has been a short circuit in the energy somewhere. There is too much energy in one part of the psyche, not enough in another part. By looking at this dream image, one can understand that the energy is being blocked off, and it is not available to consciousness. This results in depression.

The dream can tell you exactly what the problem is and even where in the body, months before a doctor could have diagnosed it. The image does not usually come as a picture of the body, but as a symbol—a car, a house, a tree. Often the soul manifests as a plant or a tree which is broken or endangered somehow.

Tarrytown: How do you work with dreams?

Woodman: First we identify a positive dream image and then we feed it to the body via the imagination. For example, a woman dreams of a beautiful flower. I ask her to picture that flower inside her body—in a place that she experiences as "dark," usually the uterus or feminine organs. When she does this, she generates energy in this area.

This is liable to make her sick in the beginning. If she has never had consciousness in that place, the energy may be too great. She may become nauseous or dizzy. Yet this difficulty passes once she recognizes her body is carrying her through a profound initiation. It is leading her to her own individual path in life.

Tarrytown: Is this a completely new way of working?

Woodman: Not entirely. The Eastern sages knew about the relationship of symbols to the body. You can see it in their description of the chakras. But in our culture, there is a failure of imagination. We confuse spiritual or soul food with actual material food. As a result, the soul is left starving and the body is abandoned.

We also don't feed ourselves images that are healthy. The images of war and violence we see on television are actually soul-destroying. But more fundamentally, the soul is not being fed because people can't receive.

Tarrytown: So we've lost a sense of communion between the body and the soul?

Woodman: Yes. For me body work is soul work and the imagination is the key to connecting both.

To have healing power, an image must be taken into the body on the breath. Then it can connect with the life force, and things can change— physically and psychologically.

A man might come into therapy and say, "I can't cry." Yet if I ask him to breathe in a symbol of his grief the tears will start. A woman may say, "I can't express my anger." But if I ask her to image this anger and then breathe it in, in a very few sessions, she may be experiencing her rage uncontrollably. That's why it's important to do this work with someone. It can be frightening on your own.

Most of us keep our breath as shallow as possible because the eruption of feeling is too intense if we inhale deeply. Breathing is very important because it is a matter of receiving and that is the feminine principle incarnate.

Tarrytown: Is our fear of rejection related to our breathing?

Woodman: Yes. If, for example, a person has an intense negative mother complex, this often manifests in a plugged throat, plugged nose, sinus trouble, asthma and all kinds of difficulty.

Sometimes in body work, the mucous starts to pour out—it oozes out in ropes, out of the eyes, the nose and the mouth—when the complex is releasing! This often signals the end of asthma and related diseases.

Such people often cannot give you their chest if you offer to hold them. They will arch. But when they start to trust, their body will begin to free itself and they will be capable of a full embrace.

However, as you solve these problems you often encounter new ones. The whole vaginal area is related to the throat and the breath. So if you release something here, you also release energy at the other end. Then you're dealing with a problem that is sexual.

Tarrytown: Can you tell us how?

Woodman: Women may find themselves with vaginal problems when they are in an incestuous relationship. The body may be saying, "Get him out of here! I want an adult male for a partner. I don't want to play little girl to my son-father anymore." The body recognizes the truth of the relationship before the psyche does. It will force you to move to a new level if you listen.

Tarrytown: What does this tell us about honoring a woman's sexuality?

Woodman: Sexuality will be crippled if a mother does not learn to love her little daughter's body. When she grows up, she may want a man to be her mother. Ann Landers asked her women readers whether they preferred to make love or to be held. Seventy per cent said they wanted to be cuddled by their husbands. But when a man has to be both mother and lover, it emasculates him.

Meanwhile, men are no more mature. Full sexuality is pretty rare in our culture. Most of us are little boys and little girls, floundering around, trying to get out of our incestuous relationships with mommy and daddy. Why? Because we have no real contact with the feminine.

Tarrytown: What signs do you see of this deprivation?

Woodman: The need for feminine recognition of the body comes up in dreams of lesbianism. When the female body has not been loved by a woman—the mother—the psyche tries to fill that gap. Often these dreams involve the analyst who is serving as a mother figure.

Once the body experiences trust in the mother's love—in dreams or life experience—it can surrender its unconscious defenses. Then it can move to a different plateau of sexuality whether in homosexual or heterosexual relationships.

Tarrytown: Are our bodies trying to teach us how to live as women?

Woodman: They certainly are. Take premenstrual syndrome for instance. A lot of women find their bodies swelling up with water. If you look at that symbolically you see the body filling up with the unconscious. In the olden days, women would have gone to the menstrual hut and looked inward, stayed with the unconscious, listened to the body. and brought this wisdom back to the tribe. But in our culture, there is no time given, no respect paid to that period.

It's like the dark of the moon. When we menstruate there has been a death. A child will not be born. But there is the possibility of new spiritual life, and evidence of our capacity to nourish it. If we don't take time to respect these mysteries, we feel a terrific tension. The body swells up and says, "Come down into my healing waters and I'll give you the symbols which will make it possible for you to go out into new life, into a new cycle."

Tarrytown: Why haven't we been more sensitive to the female body and to these warnings?

Woodman: One of the problems is the taboo against death in our Western culture. People just don't want things to die. They are afraid to let go of the old and go on with the new. The true feminine knows life is cyclical, that the caterpillar must die for the butterfly to emerge. We all must experience this chrysalis stage periodically.

Women have such potential to bring into the world a totally new insight into the cyclical pattern of life. But if they keep trying to run that straight line of perfection and performance, the body catches up with them. And the body will only be outraged for so long before it takes revenge.

Tarrytown: What happens when we don't use the body fully?

Woodman: We are disconnected from soul, from the purpose of our lives. Life is a matter of incarnation—the soul is an entity we have to live with in our human body. The problem is too many people in our culture try to skip over this step and go straight up into spirit.

Overspiritualization is a real danger, but usually the body starts to scream. People may get symptoms or an addiction. Then they can start coming down to earth again.

The anorexic men I'm working with are really worse off than the women because they are such disembodied spirits, just barely on the ground. They are magnificent people, but they don't want to be incarnated. I just keep trying to bring them into the body and into the feminine side where they can accept life.

We have got to face the agony and the ecstasy of being human—something we are not too good at in this culture. Many people don't want to be human; they'd rather live on idealization and perfection. They don't want to take responsibility for their lives because it's much easier to fly off into spirit and try to live out an archetypal dream.

Psychologically we call this *inflation* and the only end is to crash down to earth—or to recover earth—through depression or illness.

Tarrytown: Has our overly masculine culture been seduced by ideas and left the body far behind?

Woodman: Yes. But I am not at war with patriarchy. I think the world had to go through a patriarchal stage. There had to be certain "Thou shalt nots" and we needed them in the early stages of our civilization, just as children need them.

I see patriarchy as the power principle, not as genuine masculinity. It's Bully Father on the archetypal level. It is Jehovah, Father Law. Father Law upholds Mother Society, Mother Convention, Mother Church, Mother Social Insurance. Yet these two archetypes leave us with a view of our own humanity that is very incomplete and immature.

Tarrytown: How can we grow toward maturity?

Woodman: I see the world as going through an initiation into puberty. People are no longer willing to live by thou-shalt-nots. We are coming into something completely new: a new femininity balanced by a new masculinity. The Goddess is coming to light. She is coming through the Earth and through our physical bodies, but we have to relate to her with our own individual consciousness. Otherwise we could be sucked back into unconscious matriarchy.

Tarrytown: What is the positive feminine that we're moving toward?

Woodman: Love is the essence of feminine consciousness—in men and women. It is the recognition and acceptance of the total individual, and loving the individual for who he or she is. The feminine is the loving container of all conflict, all physical and psychological processes. They must not be rejected, but safely, lovingly contained. Suffering and conflict are the only way to grow. As life moves from phase to phase, you have to suffer the death of one and the birth of the next.

Tarrytown: Tell us more about this rite of passage.

Woodman: The feminine soul is what grounds us; it loves and accepts us in our totality. Our challenge today is to embody this.

For some time now I have been seeing dreams—hundreds of dreams from both sexes—about big dark women. They appear as dancers, magnificent gypsies, a Portuguese cook or people they met in the Bahamas. These great wonderful black women are a redeeming symbol. They are a saving image because they have contact with the body, and they also have a love for it. They are reminiscent of the Black Madonna, the dark earthy virgin who was worshiped in the Middle Ages and is still worshiped in many European countries today.

Tarrytown: Can individuals find wholeness if they adopt a new attitude toward the body and the life force in it?

Woodman: In part. We receive life through the orifices of the body: the eyes, ears, nose, the pores of the skin, our sexuality. If we can *really* see and hear and sense, we are continually growing.

Illness, on the other hand, may be an indication of blocked emotion. Jung called cancer a disease of despair, arthritis a disease of silent rage. Skin problems may indicate conflicts that are very close to consciousness. If the problem is profoundly deep and a long way from consciousness, it may manifest in the bowel. So you see, if we are not aware of what we're feeling, the body will exaggerate it.

Tarrytown: The irony is that our culture has paid great attention to physical fitness but without gaining any new awareness of the body.

Woodman: Whether all this emphasis on fitness machines and running and so on brings the person into greater consciousness of the body, I wonder. Running, for example, does bring lots of oxygen into the body and like many addictions gives a sense of euphoria. I think some people can run and be very much in contact with their body, while others are just running away from everything. A person using an exercise machine could be entering an intuitive communication process or fashioning armor. Some people can do exercise and they're just putting their arms through the air. Other people are moving from the solar plexus with the breath so that the entire body is coming alive. That is a soul experience. Some people dance and it's mechanical technique; other people dance and it's prayer. It depends whether consciousness is inside or outside the body, or just in the head.

Tarrytown: What happens when the body is finally listened to?

Woodman: It becomes eloquent. It's like changing a fiddle into a Stradivarius. It gets much more highly attuned. As it becomes more sensitive, it protests against all manner of psychological and physical poisons coming in. It may want different foods.

When people listen to the body, they also develop an acute sensitivity to nature. I have had men and women come into my office crying over a tree that has been cut down, a bird that has been hurt. Once you come into contact with the pain of your own body and its devastation, you become more aware of the ravages of nature.

You also recognize the agony of others who are not living in their bodies. You can see the body twisting and turning and trying to send up messages.

Tarrytown: How long does this process take?

Woodman: I tell the people I work with to give the body an hour a day and really listen. If you're not worth an hour a day, there's nothing the body can tell you and nothing I can really do.

Tarrytown: When you begin this dialogue with the body, are there different levels of communication?

Woodman: Yes. Let me give you an example. At menopause women may be given pills to keep their rite of passage at bay. If, however, they listen to their own body, it finds a way of bringing about genuine transformation—psychically and physically. The pills work for awhile but then the body finds a way of getting its message through.

The body will keep sending messages from different layers as you reach different levels of awareness. I've seen obese people lose a hundred pounds. But if they haven't dealt with their inner conflict fully, the body may break out in rashes. The interface is still wrong between the inner need and the outer attitude.

Warning signs are to be heard and obeyed. Rather than being ignored, starved, gorged or made drunk, the body must be attended to. When the body is fully open, we can trust our own feelings and actions; they anchor us in an inner home. The body protects and guides us—its symptoms are the signposts that reconnect us to our own lost soul.

2
Worshiping Illusions*

Parabola: The title of one of your books, *Addiction to Perfection,* raises a great many questions. I wonder if you could explain a little about what that title means.

Marion Woodman: Well, it comes in part from the situation in which parents have a concept of what the perfect child would be—perfect athlete, perfect scholar, when 100 percent achievement is the goal. The parents are trapped by this ideal, and their whole life is centered around performance. The child then learns how to perform and has an idealized vision of what he or she should be. Anything that doesn't fit in with that ideal has to be pushed back, has to be annihilated. As a result, whatever is human in the child, whatever is "dirty"—sexuality, and the plain, ordinary world of the body—the child experiences as not part of the perfect ideal. Spontaneity—just the natural anger or natural joy even, or the natural love of rocks and mud—is blocked, and the child gets the idea on some level that he or she is unlovable. "Whoever I am in the reality of my being is not lovable," the child concludes.

Natural being is repressed, and performance becomes everything. In any given situation a person subject to this repression will figure out whom to please and then perform in order to please that person, and their own reality is not present in the performance. People begin to live for an ideal—there's nothing else to live for. But if you are living for an ideal, and driving yourself as hard as you can to be perfect—at your job or as a mother or as the perfect wife—you lose the natural, slow rhythm of life. There's just a rushing, trying to attain the ideal. The slower pace of the beat of the earth, the state where you simply *are,* is forgotten.

P: It was forgotten long ago, really.

MW: Long ago. The parents have forgotten it, and the grandparents have forgotten it. It's a cultural situation. In its worst form, it's what happened in Nazi Germany. They sought to create a race of supermen, and they were guided by an ideal of this kind. Anything that did not fit in with that rigid

---

* Reprinted from *Parabola, The Magazine of Myth and Tradition,* vol. 12, no. 2 (Summer 1987). The interviewer was Lorraine Kisly, editor and co-publisher of *Parabola.*

concept was killed. I am now in the position to hear the dreams of people suffering from subjection to this kind of ideal, and their dreams are full of Nazi concentration camps. They are living their lives in a Nazi concentration camp. In these dreams, soldiers are killing all the women, baby girls are being raped, animals and women are having their limbs torn off. You see, the instinct is being distorted as well.

In the feminine side of our being is a much slower, less rational side, a part that moves in a much more spontaneous, natural, and receptive way, a part that accepts life as it is without judgment.

For me, perfection is a patriarchal word that splits everything into contraries: black or white. You are then living in constant conflict, and integration is not possible. Even the language is split. I find people who cannot endure words such as *masculine* and *feminine*. They go into a rage at the word *masculine* or *penetration*, or a phrase like *phallic thrust*, because they have been so outraged by what they call "the masculine principle." I don't call it the masculine principle; I call it the power principle—that's what it really is. But certainly, in the patriarchy of the business world and in many homes, what's operating is power—"You be as I want you to be," and "I love you so much that I know exactly what you ought to be," and "You will do it, or I will not accept you. I will reject you." And so people are living in terror of rejection.

P: It leads to compulsive behavior, and then the fury at the denial of most of themselves is projected back out onto their parents?

MW: Or onto men, or onto the culture. People think of the culture as being violent—they have a great fear of violence. Of course there is real violence in the streets, but the violence is inside as well. People are afraid that if they let out their rage they would actually destroy other people. So they muffle it, and secretly collude as they watch violent films, even the news.

P: Is the root of this situation a mental one? It seems to come from an idea in the mind that compels people to live according to a certain picture of themselves.

MW: It's an image of what life should be but is not. So it's worship of an illusion. It simply is not real. You can see that with an anorexic, for example. She has an image of what her body should be, and she treats herself as a Nazi would have treated her in a concentration camp. She kills her femininity in order to force herself into a rigid ideal, which is delusion.

P: The taking in of this ideal from the outside is so destructive to the individual, and yet it is taken in and embraced with gusto. Why do we embrace it if it is so self-destructive and causes so much suffering?

MW: If you are raised in a home that is based on the power principle, that's the only reality you know. You have no other world to judge by. Terrified of being left alone, the only reality you understand is pleasing other people, and you have within yourself no individual standpoint. You don't even know such a thing exists—that's the tragedy. And then you treat other people the way you were treated, so you raise your kids the same way. You know it's all wrong, that essentially you are not happy, but you have no other model for reality, so the pattern is repeated.

P: Is there anyone who is really free from this? No matter what, the parent will always have some idea of what the child ought to be like.

MW: Well, I'm sure there are some parents who can love the child for who the child is.

P: They would have to be parents who have been able to love themselves.

MW: That's right. That's where it starts. You have to forgive yourself first for being human, because to be human is to have lots of faults; so you have to forgive, and then the love flows in.

P: That's interesting because our next issue is entitled "Forgiveness."

MW: It's the crucial word. If you are brought up on ideals but know you have human failings and unacceptable qualities, you have to forgive yourself for being human, and it is through this forgiveness that you forgive others. But that is so difficult to do in our society, because we are not being loved for ourselves so we hide our worst faults.

Even in analysis, we will hide our worst faults, and if we begin to sense that we are being loved, even with all our ugliness and darkness, there is an immense fear and resistance, because we feel vulnerable, and suddenly the word *trust* starts to come in. And we are terrified of trust; we are terrified to make ourselves vulnerable. So the move into forgiveness is an immense leap. People will move to a point of trust, and then the unconscious reaction is one of terror, because they are wide open, they can be struck down. So then you have to wait. And there's another opening to more love, and then again the terror comes in. And it's the body that's terrified. Many people begin to realize at that point that their body was rejected. If they engage in depth massage or inner work in the body, the agony of the body begins to come up.

P: I'm trying to envisage this process going on outside of analysis. Could it? In a relationship with someone, for instance? So often the situation is unconscious; how do you begin to shed light on it?

MW: Many of the letters I receive are from people who are not in analysis, but they say, "Thank God for this light on what I'm trying to do. I could never see the meaning of what I was trying to do, but now I think I have some idea." They are beginning to realize that they live trying to please others. They are trying to start to live from who they are, what their needs are, what their real fears are, what their real emotions locked in their muscles are. They are trying to experience themselves as body and soul, so that others will have to respond to them in their own reality. And that takes love.

You may not like what the person is saying to you at all, particularly if you have thought of them in a certain way and all of a sudden they start saying things they never said in their lives before. If, for example, they start expressing rage or contempt, it can be very threatening. But I think that's where it starts. The person acts more and more from his or her own individual standpoint. Now that standpoint will change constantly. Gradually you become conscious of the emotions in the body supporting what you are saying, and you experience them as having substance. Instead of just speaking from the neck up, you discover what's in the body. It seems a lot of people are cut off at the neck, so they talk from the head. Meanwhile, something completely different can be going on below the neck. There's a real split inside.

P: What you have called "inner civil war."

MW: Yes, inner civil war. And that's why so many people try to drown themselves in the addiction. As soon as the rage begins to come up, they start eating or drinking or spending money, or they turn to sex or an obsessive relationship. Or gambling, or TV. Anything that will block out consciousness. The addictive substance acts as a soporific, and gradually they sink into unconsciousness.

From my point of view, in each case you have to try to figure out what the addictive substance means symbolically. Otherwise, it will hold an almost religious significance. Now that most people do not have a religious focus, the religious focus will go on to something material. They may think it's food they want, for example, because they experience themselves as starving. Well, the soul is starving; it's true, because it's not being recognized, and it's being continually starved. They then try to feed it with food, which usually symbolizes the loving mother who can accept them as they are.

P: You see different substances as having different symbolic meanings? Alcohol?

MW: Spirit, the longing for the light; whereas food grounds you, puts you back in the body, alcohol initially takes you into light. I think the positive side of addiction is that many addicts are profoundly religious people. They have immense energy, and they are not satisfied with the world as it is. They think it is a dreadfully cruel, ruthless place, and they want meaning in their lives.

P: So perhaps they feel the need more acutely than others.

MW: Because they have such a driving energy. And they want a god. Now they'd never say that, but they want something bigger than the bread-and-butter world. If that's all there is, it's meaningless. If life is nothing more than driven work, for example, it is not worth living. The alcohol takes them out of the mundane world, temporarily—and then, of course, ultimately it takes them into unconsciousness.

P: It has always seemed to me that addiction had the elements of both avoidance and substitution.

MW: Yes. The avoidance would be the avoidance of the inner civil war, and it's also an avoidance of reality. Reality is too painful if the bottom line is that I am not lovable, that I will be rejected if I am who I am. That is an unbearably painful recognition.

P: But different from the need for another level that you just spoke of?

MW: Yes. One side of it is fear. The other side is substituting an addiction for a deeper reality.

P: In your book you write that many people are driven to addiction because "there is no collective container for their natural spiritual needs."

MW: It used to be there in the church, for example, where people would enter into the sacred world, surrender to it, leave the sacred world, and take that energy back to the profane world. But they had something to take with them; they had a meaning. Their suffering was given meaning. You can't live with meaningless suffering. So you have avoidance—addicts do not live in the here-and-now. They are always going to stop drinking next Monday, or they're going to stop eating next Monday, but meanwhile eat as much as they can between now and Monday. Everything is going to be all right in the future . . . but here and now? They are never where they are; they are always running, or dreaming about the wonderful past, or the wonderful future. So they are never in the body. The body lives in the present. The body exists right now. But an addict is not in the body, so the body suffers. Uninhabited. And there's where that terrible sense of starvation comes from. To be in the now is to be full.

P: The fact that the whole culture is in an addictive state interests me in terms of this lack of meaning. It is as though there is a fundamental human need for meaning that can be as strong as instinctive needs. What could meet that need for those who are alienated from the traditional churches?

MW: Well, I think there are two things here. If you imagine the uninhabited body as sort of an empty hole, you see people try to fill it in different ways. But the soul in the body is left empty. My answer to that is that the real food of the soul is metaphor. The whole world of dreams is a metaphorical, symbolic one. Religion is based on symbol. Art, music, poetry, the whole creative world—the world of the soul—is based on it.

P: So there is a faculty within that understands this world—that lives on it, in fact.

MW: It lives on it—it is as important as food. We simply must have access to that symbolic realm, because we are not animals only, and we are not gods, only. Somehow there has to be a bridge between the animal and the divine within, and that is the symbol. Children understand this. They love fairy tales, for example. But in our culture, these are taken away from them very early on. The world of the imagination is repressed, and the soul is left crying.

P: There is an enormous price to pay to keep all of that down.

MW: It won't be held down. Eventually you'll be faced with nightmare. Eventually it will come up. Or it will take a perverse route and say, "Give me spirit," and instead of understanding this symbolically, people interpret it concretely: and they start to drink alcohol, which is a concretization of that longing.

P: There's something very hopeful in it when you look at it that way!

MW: I like working with addicts, because they are desperate and they know there is something really wrong. A lot of them wish they were dead. They are on a self-destructive course and they know it. The world as it is is intolerable, and their lives are intolerable because they aren't really living their own lives. But they *know* it. They are *right*.

P: It seems like more than a problem to fix. It seems to have a very creative aspect.

MW: It does. Death and resurrection. And they do go through the death. What I see in a broader sense is that the feminine principle, which for centuries has been so denied in our culture, is forcing its way, her way, back in again. If you're an addict, you have got to come to terms with the feminine principle. You've got to feel that slow rhythm—the rhythm of the earth is slow—you have to feel that slowing down, you have to quiet the soul, and you have to surrender, because eventually you have to face the fact that you are not God and you cannot control your life.

P: Something has to surrender; something has to let go and give up.

MW: Power—the desire to control.

P: Now, in most of us who are power possessed, the instincts governed by our feminine side are pretty primitive. Whatever is repressed in childhood is not very developed. So it comes out in very violent ways—at first, or forever?

MW: At first it will come out in very primitive ways, very challenging ways, and you will find yourself acting like a three year old: "These are my rights." People who are trying to find themselves can have very bad manners. If they were in their polite persona, they would never act that way. When that little girl starts to come out, she is wild. But she has to come out.

P: So the feminine is not just the slow benevolent rhythms of the earth— there is also the dark side of the feminine.

MW: The dark side of the feminine is vicious; it's a killer.

P: The devouring mother, Kali . . .

MW: Yes and no. Men are terrified of her—and so are women. And that side comes up—that's what's so complicated—that side comes up along with the loving, Great Mother. If you're trapped in the devouring mother, you are literally paralyzed. You wake up in the morning, and your body doesn't want to move. Here we have the Medusa that turns people to stone. If they try to do anything creative they become frozen. Or petrified. And that's real. For many people who are trying to do something from themselves for the first time in their life, as soon as that urge is felt and they really start to make a move, the dark mother appears and there is an immense battle. But you have to keep talking to her, and realize what's happening, and not give up. It takes courage and strength.

P: What is it in people that can face all of those things? The ego is involved in the repression. Is it the ego that can see what is going on? What is it in us? Obviously we have the capacity to do it.

MW: Yes. It would be ego ultimately. But most people have to work very hard to build an ego. Most people are operating in the persona, which is the showpiece, the masquerade. They are performing—they aren't in touch with their real feelings, and in a given situation, they don't know if they are angry or if they want to cry. They are unhappy about not being able to express their emotions and also terrified to do so, because expressing them has led to rejection.

P: So the ego is really the vehicle of consciousness?

MW: It is ego that can recognize what the feelings are, what the inner needs are. From a Jungian point of view, the unconscious is like a vast sea where all the complexes are floating around like onions: mother, father, hero, young child. On the underside is the collective unconscious, on the upper side is the collective in the world, and at the heart of all this there is a pinpoint called the ego, which is trying to filter what's coming through from the unconscious while at the same time trying to deal with the collective. The ego is a filter system that relates to all of reality. But considering the immense buffeting that it's getting from both the unconscious and consciousness, it has a difficult job. It takes a lot of patience to build a strong ego. But the stronger the ego is and the more flexible it is, the more it can allow to come through from the unconscious—and that's where the real wisdom is. But ego is partly in the unconscious and partly in consciousness. It tells us what is real and what is not real. If you didn't have an ego, you might think you were Christ, for example. If the place of the ego is taken over, one becomes possessed.

Actually that is what happens in an addictive state—you become possessed, and the ego is not strong enough to prevent this from happening, even though you know you are destroying yourself. There isn't sufficient ego strength to resist. So the complex takes over. But even there, it could be that the complex is acting out of a longing for the light, or consciousness. The possession that drives toward food can be a yearning for conscious femininity. The repressed energy of the feminine can no longer be caged. We are living in a global village and power alone won't work any more. We will destroy ourselves. I have enough faith to believe that the feminine is forcing her way into consciousness by means of these addictions. It changes lives, and it could change the whole culture.

P: We were just talking about how there are two aspects of this feminine force, positive and negative.

MW: When I'm talking about the feminine, I'm not talking about a mother principle. Certainly the Great Goddess is a part of this archetype—she is matter, the body. But symbolically the mother principle is based on a full breast giving to a hungry child. The mother has to give, and the child has to take. And this experience, too, can become contaminated by the power principle. Many children fall into an immense guilt, because they don't want to take. But if the mother has identified with the mother principle, the child has to take from her, or else, who is she? The feminine principle, however, is not limited to that.

P: What you just described is a distortion of the feminine?

MW: Well, it's unconscious. No mother would admit she is operating on a power principle when she's giving milk to her baby. And on the one hand she isn't, she's nourishing. But if the stage is reached where the child no longer needs her and says "Look, I don't want your orange juice," and the mother is annihilated by that, then power, or the need for control, is involved. And that causes a distortion of the mother-child relationship, because the child is trapped in guilt.

Feminine consciousness rises out of the mother, and you have to be grounded in that, because without it you'd just be blown away by spirit. Feminine consciousness, as I see it, means going into that grounding and recognizing there who you are as a soul. It has to do with love, with receiving—most of us in this culture are terrified of receiving. It has to do with surrendering to your own destiny, consciously—not just blindly, but recognizing with full consciousness your strengths, your limitations.

It gets into a much broader area, because a man's body is also feminine—all matter is feminine. We are talking archetypally about two complementary energies—we are not talking about gender. Men are even farther out of their bodies than women, it seems to me. I've seen men in body workshops where a relaxation exercise is being tried, and the men's bodies are so often terribly rigid—to the point where they cannot lie flat on the floor, the muscles are chronically locked—trying so hard to be good little boys. They can't let the muscles relax. If you think of matter as an aspect of the feminine principle, another dimension is revealed in the male body.

P: The masculine principle—or spirit—can't live anywhere except in the body. It has to be received by something.

MW: Exactly—it has to be received. And there's where consciousness comes in. You can't put spirit into dense matter. Matter is dark; it's obtuse. There has to be a consciousness to receive spirit. The way I'm understanding it—more and more from dreams—is that consciousness exists in matter, and that consciousness opens to receive spirit.

P: It develops in the process of being open to the materiality of my body, and emotions, and thoughts, and so on?

MW: By being aware of it, yes, and also by being aware of the symbol. The symbol brings the process to consciousness.

P: Where did the power principle come from? Is it a distortion of spirit?

MW: Very distorted—and we have to remember that women are trapped in this power principle just as much as men. Matriarchs are very often more authoritarian than men. What I would say is that in the hero-consciousness of the Greeks, the hero was fighting unconsciousness and trying to get a little glimmer of consciousness. For two thousand years there has been an attempt to become more and more conscious, and the hero archetype has ruled in the Western world. St. George and the dragon, for example.

P: But you're not speaking of a very developed, complete form of consciousness, are you?

MW: No, because the hero myth became contaminated by an unconscious desire for power. In terms of the evolution of our culture, the worship of goddesses in the prehistoric past gradually shifted to the worship of gods— a movement from lunar to solar consciousness. Now what's happening is that people are conscious of the power of the mother and the father complexes, and they are saying, "Who am I?" We are moving into an adolescent period, leaving behind the power principle in those two archetypes. We are trying to move into what in an individual life looks like adolescence; adolescents are pretty confused. They are dependent on the parents, and they don't want to be. And we are trapped by the complexes. We know what we're trapped in, and we want to get out. So we keep falling back in, and pulling out. That conflict is going on. It happens in the individual as he or she matures, and I see it in terms of the macrocosm as well.

P: So you see this as a critical point in history.

MW: Absolutely; if we don't make the critical transition into adulthood, we may very well destroy ourselves. We are adolescents with a hydrogen bomb and without a sense of the love that can use that energy creatively. However, addictions, personally and collectively, can keep us in touch with the god. In AA, for example, the first thing you have to admit is that you can't control your desire for alcohol, and you have to surrender to a higher power. At the point of vulnerability is where the surrender takes place—that is where the god enters. The god comes in through the wound. If you've ever been an addict, you know that you can always be an addict again, so it's at that point that the energy, if opened to, becomes available again and again.

P: Something has to give up in order for that to come in.

MW: Yes, here again we are back to the idea of consciousness in the body that has to open to spirit.

P: We spoke of addiction, for example to alcohol, where the alcohol represents on a low level the spirit. What happens when the addiction is taken away? Where does it go?

MW: I do think it's possible, with an addiction, to start living life in terms of negatives: "I won't drink." And the danger, with some alcoholics, is that they get stopped on "I will not drink." But they can't live their life on those terms. They are still obsessed with alcohol—it's still going on. It's true of any kind of addict. You may stop the addictive behavior, but as long as your mind is in that rut, it's still trapped.

P: So the surrender to a higher power needs to continue, the openness needs to go beyond the initial phase of stopping the addictive behavior.

MW: Yes, and I think AA members understand this very well—you have to go through those Twelve Steps. The addictive person has to keep working at it every day. That's what I mean about addiction keeping you in close contact with the god. You have to be very careful not to fall into some other addiction. One needs to hold that container open and live life rich and full. Otherwise you regress. There's no such thing as stasis.

P: And yet there seems to be a tremendously strong wish to stay where one is, not to move. Why?

MW: It's fear. You see in addicts the compulsion, or the wish, to keep things fixed. They are natural lovers of ritual. They create their own rituals, and the addiction will take place around that ritual. But it's a perverted ritual—it carries them into unconsciousness instead of into consciousness, because the wrong god is at the center. A ritual should take you into a much broader, richer experience; every time you go through a ritual you should contact that deepest, divine part of yourself and open to something new. If the ritual leads you into unconsciousness, you regress and become more and more deeply trapped in rigidity. If you have no personal stand-point and no boundaries, you don't dare to open.

P: It's almost as though there is an ontological imperative to grow—and if you don't, as you say, there is no standing still, only regression.

MW: Even into death.

P: I think as people get older, it starts to become evident that either they become more developed or they become caricatures of themselves. It seems that many people are suffering from a refusal to grow.

MW: We're back to the fear of annihilation again. People are terrified of death. But their terror *is* death. They turn to stone.

P: So they'll commit suicide first.

MW: They will, unconsciously. Life is a series of deaths and rebirths. You outgrow patterns, you outgrow people, you outgrow work. But if you are frightened and don't have a flexible personality, when you have to face the death of what you've always known, you are pitched into terror. That's where the addiction will really hit. Some people will cure themselves of an addiction, and then ten years later their husband or wife will die, and they have to go on to a new life and they are terrified. They have to retire, or they have to go to a new job, and the fear comes in. Well, they have to let the past die and move into a new life, or they may turn to the old addic-tion. And the addiction will throw them into unconsciousness. They can't make the move forward, so they fall back into the addictive pattern.

Often they repeat their own birth pattern. You can think of the birth canal as a transition in which you say good-bye to the womb and good morning to new life. When people enter that "canal," where the past is dead and the new not yet born, they may repeat their original birth trauma.

P: This is different for different people?

MW: Oh, of course. People who are born prematurely will try to go ahead of themselves: they'll always be two or three steps ahead of where they re-ally are. Cesarean births tend to fear confrontation. People whose mothers were drugged are the ones most likely to fall into an addiction. They tend to be quite passive—they wait for someone to do something at a moment of difficulty. But the fear is the outstanding thing, and it can manifest in bodily symptoms.

P: How, in that state of terror, does one hold oneself open, realizing that it's simply one part, not all of you?

MW: It's very important to realize it's only a part. And I think that most people in those birth passages do need support. It's very painful, and a really good friend, or several, can help—even though you have to do your own work alone.

P: This is only one part of really difficult and serious work on oneself that needs to go on. I think it is carried on in living religious traditions and, in recent times, partly in analysis. But analysis is expensive, and many people today feel estranged from religion. How much of this serious work can go on outside of a structure and without contact with someone who knows more than you do, who is more developed than you are? Can a person on their own go very far toward this openness? The world around us doesn't seem to be of much help.

MW: Well, it's an amazing thing, but when one person makes the breakthrough, a movement starts in others. I think there is such a thing as a cultural move toward consciousness. Certainly when one person in a room is more conscious, it changes the consciousness of everyone in that room. And in a family, if one person is working at becoming conscious, everyone in the household is going to be changed.

Something is happening on a large scale—there are radical changes in male-female relationships, and there is an enormous interest in spirit and matter in the fields of science, psychology, biology. I think many people are doing a lot of inner work; they are really trying to understand what is going on inside themselves. A lot of people are using dance to try to connect with the body. There is an interest in painting, in creating for the sheer joy of it. More and more people are trying to save nature from patriarchal exploitation. I know many people who are keeping journals, writing down their dreams and reconnecting with their inner self. They are questioning and trying to become conscious. No matter how they are doing it, they are contacting the symbolic world. That's how I see it. And without that, the addicts are right, life isn't worth living.

3
The Object in Analysis*

When an artist enters analysis with me and brings me some of his or her work, I do not look at it as a work of art. It belongs to the psyche and it is saying something about the condition of the psyche. Art may also be saying something about the state of the artist's psyche, but that is not its intention.

What then is its intention?

Its intention, so far as I understand it, is to say something about art, about the way in which a psychological situation is transformed into an aesthetic situation. I do not read a work of art as the enactment of a psychological problem. I do not read it to gain some clue to the artist's inner state at the time he or she made it. In analysis, however, that is the only way I read a work which the artist presents to me in the context of his or her problem.

Do you then interpret the work as a problem?

Interpretation may be too strong a word. One of the worst things that can happen in analysis is to put a label, particularly a textbook label, on the analysand's problem. In analysis I look at a work (a drawing, a painting, a poem, whatever the analysand presents) to try to locate the energy and discover where the energy wants to go. I look at it in the same way I look at a dream. Where is the energy blocked if it is blocked (most artists enter analysis because of some creative block) and where does it want to go?

The real danger of interpreting a work is that it can fixate or arrest the symbol. What the analysand is showing me is a symbol which the analysand made but does not understand. That symbol is the container of what I, following Jung, would call a healing energy. If it is not arrested or fixed, pinned as it were to the wall like a specimen, it will gradually unfold itself. I have seen this happen over and over again, and I know how destructive a premature interpretation of the symbol can be. I think I can

---

* Reprinted from *Provincial Essays,* vol. 5 (1987). The interview was conducted by Ross Woodman, professor of English at the University of Western Ontario, London, Canada.

say, then, that I never interpret a work until the work has had a chance to interpret itself. I keep waiting for whatever follows, for whatever comes next, and what comes after that. I follow, and hopefully track, the process, by trying not to anticipate it. The psyche never ceases to surprise me. I have never in all my years of practice met the same dream twice or confronted the same work twice. It just never happens. How then could I force the psyche into some preconceived pattern? How could I possibly tell it where it wants to go?

Does an unfolding work usually offer that much information?

Jung argued that the psyche is dynamic by nature. More than that, it is purposeful, directional; it moves towards goals; it is teleological (goal oriented). Every dream is not only the unconscious working of psychic energy, but also a shaping of that energy. Every dream is structured like a Greek drama, though the structure may be partially blocked or arrested. Yet even when blocked, a dream is like a torso. You can fill out from what is there what is not there. The unconscious, that is, has a structure. Northrop Frye, for example, disagreed with Jung about the collective unconscious. He said there was no need for such an hypothesis, because what Jung attributed to the collective unconscious was not unconscious at all. It was out there in that vast world of what he called the educated imagination that constitutes religion and art. Far from being unconscious, it constituted the most public of all worlds, the world we identify with civilization and culture.

What is your argument against Frye's criticism of the collective unconscious?

When an artist comes into analysis with me because he or she is blocked, I suppose I could tell the person to visit all the art museums, all the churches, synagogues and mosques, investigate the world religions, etc., in order to find release from whatever is blocking the artist in that person. But of course that would not work, at least in my experience and my knowledge of the psyche. Coleridge put it this way: "I may not hope from outward forms to win / The passion and the life whose fountains are within." Of course the manifestations of the collective unconscious are out there in the public world of religion and culture, but unless what is out there is intimately connected to the unconsciousness of the artist (or anyone else) it is merely out there. We do not have immediate and direct access to it. By blocked I mean an artist (or indeed anyone) who experiences himself or herself as cut off, isolated, alienated. They are experiencing what Jung called loss of soul which is a universal phenomenon and for an artist a death-like, perhaps death-dealing, experience. It can lead—and in artists it often does—to suicide by a variety of means other than the more obvious ones.

So for you art therapy . . .

Let me correct you on one point. I am not an art therapist. Analysands do bring me their work, but in the same way they bring me their dreams. I am by my Jungian training what you could I suppose call a dream therapist in that I work primarily with dreams, though more and more I work almost as much with the body. But the word therapist is also inaccurate. I am not only not an art therapist, I am not a therapist. I am an analyst. I do not provide therapy, prescribe a program of healing. I listen to the unconscious and, so far as I can, let the unconscious prescribe. I treat the "art" they bring me—which I do not view as "art"—as I treat dreams. I make no real distinction. I treat the work as the language of the unconscious, both the personal and the collective unconscious. I know something about that language. Indeed I think of that language as in the most literal sense our "mother tongue." I speak that language at least eight hours a day. I dream in that language, and when I lecture I talk in that language.

Did your training as a Jungian analyst in Zürich include what is called art therapy?

There was nothing called art therapy taught in Zürich. For four years, week after week, we studied the work (drawings, paintings, sculptures) of disturbed people, a few of them institutionalized. But we did not look at it as art or think of it as art, and in most cases neither did the patients. When a patient thought of the work he or she presented as a patient (or if in analysis as an analysand} as art, that person was in serious trouble. It usually meant that he or she was deeply committed to his or her illness, had a stake in it that might be impossible to overcome.

What was the purpose of this training?

We used the work both for diagnosis and prognosis. That is, we were not told in advance the condition or the symptoms of the person who made it. Our task was to gain a fair degree of accuracy in diagnosis (one never made a full diagnosis on the basis of "art" work alone) and in prognosis.

What do you mean by prognosis?

I mean the severity of the condition, whether it was neurotic or psychotic, and what chances there were for successful treatment.

How did you distinguish between neurosis and psychosis?

In psychosis the psyche is split, severely fragmented. This condition will be indicated in numerous ways, in the partial elimination of figures, in surrounding an image with a black outline. But it is also usually possible to see not only where the energy is most highly concentrated but even sometimes where it wants to go, the direction in which it is moving, or trying to move. It is there, in the indications of direction, that a prognosis may be possible.

Can you distinguish between neurosis or psychosis and art?

Van Gogh suffered psychotic periods during his life and did some of his finest work while confined to an asylum. I have seen some of the work he did in the last phase of his life that ended with suicide. And I have read the poems of Sylvia Plath that also appear to be a rehearsal for suicide. And I know that Shelley's drowning was psychically rehearsed in an elegy he wrote on the death of John Keats. Yet I would not call any of their work that prefigures suicide (or whatever) neurotic or psychotic.

Why not?

That is not easy to answer. Freud said that great works of art cannot be successfully explained by psychoanalytical methods. Works of genius (and I use the word advisedly) transcend both neurosis and psychosis. Why or how this should be remains in part a mystery, though Jung among others offered a partial explanation. The psyche, as I suggested, is dynamic and directional. Left to itself, it will move of itself towards the gratification of its needs. That movement towards the gratification of its needs gives rise to a metaphorical rather than literal language. It gives birth to a world of symbols which have an internal coherence that may not be immediately perceived or understood. In psychosis the coherence of symbolic patterns is either destroyed or obsessively fixated in compulsive repetition. In neurosis the pattern is curiously defensive rather than open and explorative. The work is claustrophobic, fearful, imprisoned within itself. Some have seen that in the last work of Van Gogh or in some of Sylvia Plath's last poems. But if one looks at the enormous energy of the work, at the facing up to (as if in celebration of) real danger (and to that degree overcoming it), one sees, I think, that the work is the triumph over neurosis and psychosis, a movement to a larger integration, to some vaster sense of wholeness. That's what Freud had the ability to recognize in Dostoevsky, for example, and he knew there was no way to reduce it to an analysis of a neurosis or psychosis.

Could you be more specific by dealing, say, with one of van Gogh's last paintings?

I suppose the painting that has received the most critical attention is *Crows Over the Wheat Field,* which may have been his last. Most commentaries on it stress the brooding sense of menace, the three paths that end abruptly, the "no-exit" from the field, the black crows flying toward the artist-spectator that seem to extend the sky as if a dark shroud or veil were descending.

But I think that the painting can be equally read not as a closure but as an opening. The green path turning into the golden wheat field at the very center of the painting does not end. It carries the eye not toward a horizon (there is no horizon) but toward a rather precarious, unsettled blue opening. The black crows could be flying through this opening extending the path of the artist-spectator (the path of the eye) upward and out. Our hindsight knowledge of van Gogh's suicide may prejudice our reading. My suggestion is that the possible opening, flying away, is characteristic of van Gogh's larger visionary power which, however unsettling the brushwork or the palette knife, transcends illness.

There is certainly a farewell-presence in the painting (the construction of a departure), but not into madness. What some have described as a cosmic chaos is far more cosmic than chaotic. It has all the concentrated power of a genuine imminence which I would describe as a painterly struggle toward a metaphysical resolution. The psyche is carving its way toward the object of its desire. To the conscious mind governed by the ego that way can be pretty frightening. Vision, I suggest, is always either the defeat or willing surrender of the ego. In van Gogh, his whole life as an artist was one of willing surrender, the creative process understood as a psychic process. The shape of that life—the composition of the canvas— enacts a struggle to overcome the limitations of physical reality. I place that struggle at the very center of modern art.

If, however, van Gogh were in analysis with you and brought you this painting how would you read it?

I would probably ask van Gogh where each of the three roads might take him. I would ask him where the crows are going. I would, that is, encourage him to relate to his inner struggle in a non-painterly way. I would help him if I could to harness his impressive energies on the side of life by encouraging him to see that his own inner work was not yet complete, that his soul was not yet made. Ideally—and I stress ideally—one dies when one has at last entered fully into life. Then death is a kind of completion, an arrival at life. Suicide is always an interference with the process, a short-circuiting, a short-cut.

Could you not argue that if van Gogh had been in analysis with you he might not have committed suicide, but also not have painted these great paintings of his last phase?

That is the question raised in Peter Shaffer's play, *Equus*. To heal the patient is to rob him of his daimon. The play may have sensationalized the problem, but by doing that it brought it home to a lot of people. Jackson Pollack was in Jungian analysis for a time. I suspect, though I do not know, that it was of little or no help to him as an artist. Indeed, by looking at his own works which he brought to his analyst from a therapeutic point of view he may have lost touch with the kind of presence they had as art works. His return to figuration, which some considered a real falling off, even a betrayal, may have been a genuine loss when measured against those vast, all-over, drip paintings that are, I think, sublime in the full aesthetic sense of the word.

What do you mean by the word "psyche"?

Psychology means the science of the soul. The terrible irony is that many psychologists think of themselves as scientists who do not believe there is such a thing as soul. A behaviorist does not believe there is such a thing as soul. A psychology without a psyche is surely a contradiction, don't you think?

By psyche I mean the presence of the observer in the things observed, a presence that changes what is observed. When we see something 'out there' we see an image. This image is constructed at the perceptual center of the brain. The physical object does not enter the eye. What enters are the light waves (or the sound waves in the case of the ear) which become electrical impulses that the brain converts into images. The consciousness of those images as images is what I mean by soul. Soul is not the physical external thing but the immaterial image of it which may or may not have an identity with the external thing. The point is that it is not bound to the external thing. The soul is not restricted to making a copy. The world the observer constructs from the things observed is always other than the things observed. In Greg Curnoe's studio there are bicycles hanging from the ceiling that one can take down and ride.* There are also pictures of bicycles leaning on the walls that one cannot ride. If you tried to you would destroy an image.

---

* Greg Curnoe is an artist in London, Ontario.

That image, as distinct from the thing, is called in alchemy and other like-minded traditions the subtle body. It is not the thing-in-itself, but the image of it constructed by the brain and reshaped or reconstituted in an infinite variety of ways by the imagination, the image-making power of the brain. Soul is the world of metaphor. We inhabit it all the time whether we know it or not. A psychotic doesn't know it, most unconscious people don't know it. Artists do know it, and when for whatever reason they lose the metaphor-making power, can no longer write poems or paint pictures or compose music, they know it in the most intimate, immediate and painful sense. They know that unless they can recover it they as artists cannot go on living. Suicide is intimately present in the consciousness of any blocked artist with whom I have worked. They know from first-hand experience what the death of the soul is and means.

A fellow Jungian, James Hillman, wrote a book about this called *Suicide and the Soul.* There is, he suggests, a kind of metaphorical suicide enacted in the making of images, in the making of art. It consists of substituting a subtle body, an image, for the actual one. The vast majority of people have never experienced the death of the soul because they have never experienced the living soul—like the whale that has never experienced the ocean because it has never been washed up on the shore.

4

On Addiction and Spirituality*

In the early 1930s, Jung worked with one of the alcoholics, Rowland H., whose sobriety helped lead to the creation of AA. Under Jung's care for a year in Switzerland, Rowland was able to stay sober, but as soon as he returned to the U.S. he got drunk again. He returned to Switzerland, and Dr. Jung told him the only hope for him was a spiritual transformation. There was simply no "cure." Bill W. and Jung exchanged letters about this event many years later, in 1961. *** Jung pointed out that it was no accident that alcohol is also called "spirits" and said that the alcoholic's thirst for alcohol is equivalent to the soul's thirst for "the union with God."*

"Alcohol in Latin is spiritus, *and you use the same word for the highest religious experience as well as for the most depraving poison. The helpful formula therefore is:* spiritus contra spiritus," *he wrote in his January 30, letter to Bill W., in 1961. It's an alchemical formula. It takes spirit to counter spirit.*

Looking at alcoholism and addiction as a longing for spirit might mean that something very different is going on in our society. One might say that we don't have a crisis with alcohol and drugs as much as we have a spiritual crisis. Addiction is the perversion of spirit, our spiritual nature turned inside out, devouring itself. The epidemic of addiction can also be seen as spirit trying to reenter our society.

With these thoughts in mind, I went to Toronto to talk with Jungian analyst Marion Woodman about the nature of addiction, the symbol of the child, and her work.

Rachel V: In *The Pregnant Virgin* you talk about how healing has to come through the wound. That paradox reminds me of Christ's comments about how the weak will confound the strong.

Marion: The weak does confound the strong. The conscious ego may

---

* Reprinted from Rachel V., *Family Secrets: Life Stories of Adult Children of Alcoholics* (New York: Harper & Row, 1987), pp. 145-158.
** See Jan Bauer, *Alcoholism and Women: The Background and the Psychology* (Toronto: Inner City Books, 1982), appendix 3, for copies of this correspondence.

know exactly what it wants to do, may be moving right along through life in a very strong, goal-directed, ambitious way, but the unconscious, childish side of the personality can bring the ego down. Indeed, it will bring the ego down unless it is recognized.

The weak side is the addictive side, so that it is only in dealing with that childish/childlike side that the individual is ultimately able to function. The chain is as strong as its weakest link. It's that weak side that is involved with divinity as I see it. The childish part that is so uncontrollable, so demanding, so tyrannical, is at the same time the childlike part that brings joy and creativity into life. It is the soul that will not be silenced. Buried in matter, it yearns for spirit. A longing for alcohol does symbolize a longing for spirit. Think of the Greeks with Dionysus, the god of the vine. Intoxication and the transcendent experience with the god were intimately connected.

Think about the symbolism in the Christian mass where the wine becomes the blood of God and the bread the body of God, spirit and matter. Alcoholics are longing for spirit because they are so mired in matter, but they make the mistake of concretizing that longing in alcohol. Maybe if they really understood what they were longing for and could go into the realm of the imaginal, the soul's realm, then something very different could begin to happen.

What is this terrible starving in an addiction? It's as though our whole civilization is feeding the hunger, not to satisfy, but to make us hungrier. There is this sense of "I want more, more, more of—something." In eating disorders—binging, anorexia, bulimia—you find the same drivenness. Addicts do their best to discipline themselves and they may do a very good job from 7 a.m. to 9 p.m. Then they go to sleep. Their ego strength goes down and suddenly the unconscious comes up. As soon as the unconscious with all its instinctual drive erupts, the ego loses control. Then the addiction becomes a tyrant. Its voice is that of a starving, lost child: "I want, I want, I want, and I am going to have." There's an instance of the weak confounding the strong.

Rachel V: I don't know that much about anorexia and bulimia except they seem to be akin to some kind of profound rejection of the body.

Marion: Yes, a profound rejection of matter. Often you find a syndrome that goes from obesity to anorexia to alcoholism. Or it may go into religious fanaticism. Addicts tend to move from one addiction to another. So long as they are in that addictive behavior, they are just substituting one addiction for another. The healing has not taken place. Think of AA members who remain sober as long as they are workaholics. The drivenness is still operating in the household. In such situations, the children will pick up the unconscious of the parent who desperately wants a drink and runs to food or runs to work or any other addiction as a way to keep off the bottle. The child picks up that unspoken yearning, that unlived life, and the compulsive repetitiveness that expresses and escalates denial. The child in its own way tunes into what is absent in the parent and goes after it.

I think to get to the core of the problem, you've got to look at what we have done to the body, what we have done to matter in our culture. The Latin word *mater* means "mother." Mother is she who cherishes, nurtures, receives, loves, provides security. When the mother cannot accept her child in its peeing, puking, animal totality, the child too rejects its body. It then has no secure home on this earth, and in the absence of that primal security it substitutes other mothers: Mother Church, Mother Alma Mater, Mother Social Insurance, even Mother Food, which it also cannot accept. A desperate love/hate relationship develops. The terror of losing Mother equals the terror of being buried alive in her. Without the security of the body home, the individuals must rely as best they can on these substitutes for the maternal security they do not have. More than that, if the body is rejected, its destruction becomes one's modus operandi. The fear of cancer does not make an addictive personality stop smoking.

In the absence of the nourishing mother, whether personal or archetypal, people try to concretize her in things, as if to make present what they know is absent. Ironically, what they capture is not a presence that they always experience as absent but the absence itself. Think of how people try to photograph everything, tape-record it, try to capture and hold an event in a static state. That's what I mean by "concretize." Like the evil witch who turns everything to stone.

I went to see the pope in Toronto, and after he passed by, the woman in front of me burst into tears, crying, "I never saw him!" She had a camera and had been so busy taking pictures of him that she never "saw" the man she came to see. By concretizing the moment, she missed it. The person she came to see is caught in the picture, but the picture reminds her only of absence. She was absent from the experience.

Think of tourists jumping out of a bus at the Grand Canyon. They snap pictures, but they never arrive at the Grand Canyon. They don't open themselves to the experience. Inwardly they are not nourished by its grandeur. The soul in the body is not fed. It's like slides filed away in a box that no one, even you, wants to look at.

William Blake says the body is "that portion of Soul discerned by the five Senses." I live with that idea. I sit and look out my window here in Canada and the autumn trees are golden against the blue sky. I can feel their "food" coming into my eyes and going down, down, down, interacting inside, and I fill up with gold. My soul is fed. I see, I smell, I taste, I hear, I touch. Through the orifices of my body, I give and I receive. I am not trying to capture what is absent. It's that interchange between the embodied soul and the outside world that is the dynamic process. That's how growth takes place. That is life.

Most people do not feed their souls, because they do not know how. Most of us in this culture are brought up by parents who like the rest of society are running as fast as they can, trying to keep up financially, socially and every other way. There's a drivenness that the child is subjected to even *in utero*. In infancy the child is expected to perform. Often the parent isn't able to receive the soul of the child, whatever the little soul is, because the parent doesn't take time to receive or doesn't like what the child *is*. Many parents are too interested in seeing that the child will have dancing or skating lessons, a good education, and be at the top of the class. They are so anxious about all they are trying to "give" to the child that they do not receive from the child.

The child, for example, comes running in with a stone, eyes full of wonder, and says, "Look at this beautiful thing I found," and the mother says, "Put it back outside in the dirt where it belongs." That little soul soon stops bringing in stones and focuses on what it can do to please Mommy. The process of growth turns into an exercise in trying to figure out how to please others, rather than expanding through experience. There's no growth without authentic feeling. Children who are not loved in their very beingness do not know how to love themselves. As adults, they have to learn to nourish, to mother their own lost child.

Rachel V: You've talked so much about the mother and the Goddess. I need to clarify that what I think we've been talking about *isn't* male or female, but different aspects of the human experience. These are not so much issues of gender as epistemology. We are straining the language here. The verbal shorthand of associating certain qualities such as receptivity with the feminine do us all a disservice and I think compound our difficulties. "Masculine" and "feminine" are descriptions of experience, not the experience itself. Is that right? "The map is not the territory," as philosopher Gregory Bateson said. We end up with a neo-Manichean split if we're not careful. The basic premise is that we are all, men and women alike, both male and female, biogenetically as well as psychologically.

Marion: Yes, Rachel, I agree. This is not about gender, male, or female. These are archetypal energies I'm talking about.

Rachel V: The denial of feeling and the emphasis on pleasing, keeping the peace and performing is not limited to alcoholic families.

Marion: True, but I think there is some addiction in most families; our culture is addicted. The addiction can cover a broad range of problems: parents that are involved with another partner, a relationship addiction, a food addiction, gambling, sleeping, an addiction to TV, which is another way of going to sleep. I have analysands who go to sleep the minute I say anything they don't like. In five minutes, they come to. They cannot take confrontation. They cannot take pain, and as soon as they feel it coming, they fall into unconsciousness, which wipes out the possibility of growth. They cannot confront. Where there is real strength required in a spiritual confrontation or a real meeting of souls, they cannot even receive love. They are afraid of love because it makes them vulnerable.

To take that further, what you're left with is an infant, an abandoned infant inside the body. The body becomes an immense cavity with this screaming little baby inside. There is the abandoned child. On a symbolic level we might say that this is the divine child. Sooner or later that divine child starts to scream and he's the weak one that brings down the seemingly strong parts of the personality. Thus the addiction in its own circuitous way may be trying to bring us back to the God within—embodied spirit—Incarnation.

Rachel V: This idea of becoming like a child to enter the kingdom of God, do you know of other cultures where we find this image?

Marion: In the story of Persephone and Hades there is a child. Hades abducts Persephone and takes her into the Underworld, where in some versions of the myth she has a child. In many of the myths, Leda and the swan, Danae and the shower of gold, for example, the human woman is impregnated by the god. In other words, matter is penetrated by spirit and the child of the union of matter and spirit is the divine child.

What is going on then in a person who is forced to surrender, to say, "Yes, I am an alcoholic, I am an addict, I am powerless over my addiction. I have to turn myself over to a higher power"? That person is surrendering matter to spirit. There's the union that can produce the divine child. The addiction has made receptivity possible. Many of us cannot understand how powerful femininity is until we are brought to our knees through addiction or illness.

I think it's important to recognize that on some level, in some peculiar way, we're all in the same mess, whether we're alcoholic, children of alcoholics, anorexic, workaholic, or drug or money addicted. Addicts are trying to run away from God as fast as they can. Paradoxically, they are running right into her arms. Consciousness makes them realize how the soul is trying to lead them into the presence of the divine if only they can understand the symbolism inherent in the addictive substance or behavior.

Take food as the addictive object. The biggest problem in dealing with an anorexic is that once she starts to eat, stops fasting and breaks the euphoria caused by the fasting, she feels life is boring. Eventually, she has to recognize that rejecting food is rejecting the reality of being human, and her addictive behavior is the acting out of her tyrant child determined to control or escape the tyrannical parent, whether that parent is inside or outside. So the anorexic, and this is true for all addicts, has to come to a new way of life.

If you live day by day, in touch with the world around you, even a minute a day, as Blake says, then that's the moment in each day that Satan cannot find, it's what you need to keep the soul alive. Because you are in touch with the eternal, you hone into Home. Then you can *see* the bronze blue morning; you can *hear* your child's silence. Then life is never boring. Too many people never take that moment in the day, so they run around trying to find it, outside. That's the problem: they try to do it outside themselves and that hurls them into the addiction.

All the running is away from the tragic fear that we are not loved. Unless we perform well, we are not lovable. That terror leads to self-destructive behavior. It can also lead to global self-destruction. Addictions may be the Goddess's way of opening our hearts to what love is—love of ourselves, love of others, love of the dear planet on which we live.

Lots of people are trying to find spirit through sexuality. Through orgasm they think they can be released from matter; for one brief moment they hope to experience this extraordinary union of spirit and matter. But if they can't bring relationship into sexuality it's just a fly-by-night thing. Eventually it just becomes mechanical, and then they become frantic. "I've got to have it. It's got to work. It's not going to work. It's my fix." Sexuality without love is matter without spirit. People who are unable to love may be addicted to sexuality and be driven over and over again to try to find love. What they are projecting onto sexuality is the divine union they so desperately lack within themselves.

Jung said the opposite of love is not hate but power, and where there is love there is no will to power. I think this is a core issue in working with addictions. Sooner or later, the feminine face of God, Love, looks us straight in the eye, and though her love may manifest as rage at our self-destruction, she's there. We can accept or reject—live or die.

I don't know about muffins in the States, but muffins in Canada are numinous. A patient came in yesterday, a woman with an eating problem and she was crying. "I don't know what to do," she said. "You tell me I have to recognize my feelings. Most of the time I don't do anything I want to do because I don't feel it would be right. I was driving here, and I had a desire to bring you a muffin. Then I thought you wouldn't want the muffin. But I know you would love a muffin, but no I won't buy it. You don't take your analyst a muffin. But then I got into such a state, I was just sweating, because I wanted to get the muffin so much. I stopped the car, went back, got the muffin, and I have the muffin in the bag, but I don't know whether to give it to you or not. I feel such a stupid child, but I don't know what to do."

"Well," I said, "I want to receive the muffin."

I broke the muffin in two and gave her half. Because of the love that was in the muffin, and because she had been received, it was a communion. It's a simple, simple story, but I tell you, people at that level of feeling are so terrified of being rejected that a muffin can bring out the rejection of a lifetime. In outer reality this woman is most competent. She's very professional, highly respected. Everybody thinks she is very mature, and she is except for this rejected child. Here's the weak again. The little child says, "I want to take Marion a muffin." If that child has been rejected and rejected and rejected, it goes almost into a state of nonexistence. It experiences loss of soul. The person becomes disembodied. That's the point of vulnerability to an addiction. It is also the point where the god or goddess can enter.

At the heart of it is the religious issue. Our soul is our eternal relationship with God. The soul's language is the language of dreams. As I see it, every dream is a communication with God. We have an inner dialogue going on all the time. At night we experience it. But I think if we stop to daydream during the day we drop back into the dream. Periodically, we come to consciousness, then we drop back. The dream gives us symbols, images, but because we're so concretized we don't understand the symbols. We say dreams are crazy, silly. We have cut ourselves off from the world of the symbol, and so we have forgotten the language of dreams.

Thus we make the mistake of assuming that if we're uneasy, insecure, it is food that we want. Thirsty? We have to drink. Feeling a little empty in the gut? We need sex or whatever other concrete thing we can get hold of. But it is the soul that is calling out in dreams and the soul communicates through symbols. If we meditate on these images, they reach us on all levels: imaginative, emotional, intellectual. Our whole being, including our body, resonates. We feel ourselves whole. The images of that eternal world are the images of the bread-and-butter world—food, drink, sexuality. That's where the two worlds meet. That's why we have to be so careful interpreting dreams. A sexual dream, for example, may be the soul's way of expressing a need for the union of spirit and soul—some creative act such as dance, painting, writing. Alcohol as a symbol may be a need for spirit. Gallons of ice cream cannot bring sweetness to the soul, nor will gallons of gin float you into the presence of God.

Our own inner child has to be disciplined in order to release its tremendous spiritual power. If we identify with its childish side we say, "I was always a victim. I will always be a victim and it's all my parents' fault." Then we can go around with a hangdog look the rest of our lives. If on the other hand we identify with the child*like* part we say, "My parents were the victims of a culture, as were their parents and their parents. I will not be a victim. I will take responsibility for my own life. I will live creatively. I will live in the *now.* "

To be childlike is to be spontaneous, able to live in the moment, concentrated, imaginative, creative. Most of us have forgotten how to play, forgotten the joy of creativity. Without joy, we find ourselves running away from pain. Without creativity, we run away from emptiness. The faster we run, the more severe our addictions. We cannot face our own nothingness. Nothingness is the ultimate anguish of childish people who live their lives knowing who they are not rather than who they are.

In the New Testament when the divine child was born, Herod the King ordered the killing of all the babies in the kingdom. That's what happens when our own inner child is born. Herod represents the conventional collective attitudes that will be destroyed if new life thrives. As soon as our inner child comes alive and says, "This is who I am. These are my values," all the terrified Herods in our environment rise up and say, "You are a fool." If the baby is not protected, it will be killed. It takes immense courage to find out the values of our own divine child and even greater strength to live those values. Addictions drown it, starve it, drug it, try to kill it. Ironically, they keep us in touch with it as we run round and round the hole where it is hidden.

Lucifer and Christ are very close together in many addicts who yearn for a "high." A fast high. They want to be gods in control of a perfect world in which they are perfect. They long to be like Lucifer, the morning star, the brightest star, the first son of God. And like Lucifer, their pride brings them into collision with God. They cannot accept their own human imperfection. They cannot live in a universe they cannot control. When they stand in their own desert, their inner Lucifer faces their inner Christ and says, "I will give you all the power and material goods you want if you will bow down to me."

Addicts are trapped in illusions of their own power, illusions that rob them of their human life. They are driven by a voice inside, "I have to. I can't. I've got to. I won't." They long for a paradise not of this earth. They don't want to be here, but they are. Their bodies are driven, their muscles so tight they can't relax. Some addicts overcompensate by allowing the body to fall into a stupor. On a Friday night, for example, if the body is armored and tense, a woman may be saying to herself, "I will not drink, I will not," but another voice says, "I'll explode if I don't let go. I've done everything everybody wants me to do all week. No more. I'll show you who's boss. I'm going to drink and I'm going to drop out of consciousness. I don't want to feel anything."

Trying to be a god or a goddess all week can flip into being an animal all weekend. There is no *human* balance in the addict.

Rachel V: Are we ever free from an addiction?

Marion: In AA, however many years you are dry, you still say, "I am an alcoholic." How many people do you know who fell back into their trap after one drink or one cigarette? The unconscious is like the ocean: the obsession can fall deep into the ocean floor, but a crisis can bring it charging up from below.

Life moves in cycles, consciousness expands. Each time we are faced with some new truth about ourselves part of us dies and a new part is conceived. In the fullness of time we have to move through a birth canal and birth canals can be dangerous. In any experience people tend to repeat their original birth trauma each time they attempt to leave the warm womb they have cuddled into. If they were Cesarean births they may hesitate to confront; if they were breech births, they might go at things backward; if their mother was drugged, they will tend to find some anesthetic (drugs, alcohol, food) to throw them into unconsciousness. These points of transition where we are called to stretch into new maturity are the points where the addiction is most liable to resurface.

Changing the habitual behavior is extremely difficult because it is the only behavior one knows and it is interlocked with the unconscious behavior of one or both parents. If you are convinced that at some point in a relationship you will step into an ambush and fall into a dark hole, then that becomes your habitual behavior and you can be sure you will land in that ambush. You are in it before you know what is happening because it is your unconscious reaction. If you can pull consciousness in and say, "I don't have to fall into that trap," then you walk at a more cautious pace and foresee the danger. With this steady perceptive awareness, I think it is possible to reach the point of stillness that is free of the addiction.

Our culture is not geared to process. It values security and the status quo, and because we are living under the shadow of nuclear war and annihilation we try to hang onto whatever permanence we can. The pain of leaving the old life behind and facing the new without any real understanding of who we are becomes unendurable. Some cultures have rites of passage that give meaning and companionship to people in transition. Most of us experience total aloneness. I see it in dreams where the dreamer comes to a border crossing in pitch dark, confronted by fascist customs officials or has to cross a rickety bridge that spans a river of whirlpools. Addicts tend to be loners; their dark intuitions take them out of their bodies. In an ungrounded state, sheer terror can drive them back to the addiction.

Intuition can be a blessing and a curse. People who are intuitive are never quite in their bodies. They are confounded by possibilities and driven this way and that exploring what might be. They are rarely in the present, never filling their bodies. Their bodies then become vulnerable to all the pain in their environment. Through osmosis they pick up other people's unconscious garbage. When the load becomes too heavy, they escape through an addiction. (Think of this dynamic between parents and children.) Again, it is the problem of absence. The soul is hiding somewhere in the gut; it isn't animating the whole body. You feel that when addicts hug you. Their children sense it, and while they can't articulate it, they are haunted by emptiness. They feel they are living in an illusion where nothing is quite what it seems; the left hand doesn't know what the right hand is doing. Dad is charming; Dad is vicious. Mom dresses like a model; Mom is a slob.

Transitions are hell. Your beloved dies or goes away and you are left alone. That is hell, it is also an opportunity to grow. Alone, we dialogue with our own bodies, our souls. Their wisdom is exactly what we need for our own wholeness. It makes quite clear what is real, what is illusion. It strips off layers of false pride. It make us human. What a relief to be a human being instead of the god or goddess Mom and Dad projected onto us!

Each hell burns off more illusions. We go into the fire, die and are reborn. To put it in Christian terms, we carry our own cross, we are crucified on our own cross, and we die and are resurrected on a new level of awareness. We find our balance on that plateau for awhile and then another period of growth is demanded and a new cycle begins.

Addiction, like any illness, can bring us into our bodies. Healing comes through embodiment of the soul, the soul living in the here and now. The body is. The soul in matter is what I think the feminine side of God is all about. The agony of an addiction can break the heart open to the love that

is present in all creation. It is that breaking point that is so important—
that's the edge where addicts tend to live—annihilation or apocalypse. Our
technological age pushes us so fast that we annihilate what is happening
to us. We pass by the moments of soul. We move from incident to incident without being there. An anorexic in a euphoric trance can move to the
edge of death without any awareness of what is literally happening. If I
say, "Look, you're going to die," she looks at me in bland astonishment.
Unless an incident is made conscious, it does not happen in the soul. It
has to be thought about, written about, painted, danced, made into music.
In other words, it must move from literal to metaphoric if it is to be assimilated into the soul's flowering.

That's what analysis is about. As analyst, I become the mirror to reflect
back to the patient what is being said, what the body is saying, what remains silent. Without a mirror, we can't see ourselves. But one doesn't
need an analyst for reflection. Keeping a journal can provide an opportunity for reflection, for example. Parents who are locked in their own narcissistic need cannot provide a mirror for their child, and therefore the child
cannot develop an individual identity. Take the small incident of that muffin. Had we not taken time to reflect on the need and the love and the faith
epitomized in buying that muffin, we would have committed soul murder.
Such a tiny interchange seems like nothing until you remember the moments in your own childhood when you hoped and you loved and you gave
your all and nobody received you. That's death.

It happens again and again with my analysands. Their pain is so deep
that it takes a very long time for the real feeling to surface. People are
ashamed of what they call their childishness, but those blocked feelings
cannot mature if they have no one with whom to interact. So long as we
are determined to move at our swift, logical pace, the child remains hidden.
The natural rhythms of the body are slow. The little soul-bird that was put
away in a dark box in childhood needs time and silence to learn to trust
again.

5

Healing Through Metaphor*

Though the lecture hall is packed, the dim lighting lends it a sense of intimacy. Behind the rostrum, tribal masks hang alongside moon-suffused paintings of hunters, potters and shamans. This is the opening session of the 1987 "Journey into Wholeness," a Jungian-oriented conference held in the North Carolina mountains every fall.

At the lectern is keynote speaker Marion Woodman, an analyst from Toronto. Her topic for the evening is "The Wounded Feeling Function," but instead of delivering a theoretical lecture on the subject, Woodman is telling a story. Called "The Man She Never Married," it revolves around a successful professional woman's lifelong relationship with a literary scholar. It overflows with dreams, long walks on the beach and sudden insights that arrive during the most casual conversations. Throughout the story Woodman weaves her themes: individuation, healing of the feeling function, and masculine/feminine balance in the psyche.

At tomorrow's session, her comments will make it clear that the heroine's emotional dance with the man she never marries is symbolic of a woman's interaction with her own animus. But tonight, questions of symbolism remain in the background, like the masks and moonlight. The intricate plot, the charming heroine and the quietly passionate storyteller hold the audience spellbound.

Woodman is known for her studies of eating disorders and addictive behavior, and is thoroughly at home in the world of case histories and research methodology. However, she often prefers to present her psychological ideas indirectly, by telling stories. When asked about this she stresses her belief that story has more of an impact than abstract analysis.

"So long as it's theory it's removed from the actual feeling of the audience, and they can get so caught up in the words that they don't realize it's their own body I'm trying to address. If I put it in a story form or use images, the mind may not hear it, but the body responds. And if it's reverberating in the body, sooner or later it's going to get through to consciousness. I feel that it's more immediate to tell a story or to use metaphor."

In stories such as "The Man She Never Married," Woodman's goal is

---

* Reprinted from *Common Ground* (Summer 1988). Written by Ralph Earle, a free-lance writer and columnist in Pittsboro, NC.

not simply to give information about the general relationship of feminine to masculine, but to cause the listeners, through identification with the characters' conflicts, to feel that relationship within their own body, mind and psyche.

Woodman feels that the essential ingredient for this kind of direct communication is metaphor. Citing the word's Greek origin (from the verb "to transform"), Woodman sees metaphor as refining the raw energy patterns of the unconscious into forms that can be assimilated into consciousness. She feels that this transforming function is a universal feature of metaphor that works similarly in folk stories, literary works and dreams.

As an example, Woodman cites a dream in which a woman is told she should eat fish. Since "fish" is a culturally-accepted symbol for Christ, the dream implies that the dreamer needs to assimilate some kind of spiritual entity. An unconscious need of the individual has been translated into consciousness by the metaphor of the fish: the message is that spiritual energy is necessary for the ongoing balance of the psyche.

Woodman says that Jung called metaphor "the healing symbol." According to Jung, metaphor affects the person on three levels: the mental level on which we interpret meaning, the imaginative level, where the actual transforming power resides, and the emotional level connected to the feelings embodied in the metaphor. The metaphor's simultaneous operation on these three levels enables metaphor to make a deep connection to the psyche. Woodman elaborates:

"If the metaphor really hits you, it gives you goose pimples; you say, 'Ah, that's it, that's it, yes.' The whole being is momentarily brought into a sense of wholeness, and if you can hold onto that, two or three weeks later you get another metaphor that brings together that wholeness again. . . . And there is the healing process—you go from one sense of wholeness to another through the metaphors."

Full healing or transformation is not likely to occur through the work of a single story or a single dream, but the ongoing process of transformation continues as long as individuals remain open to the metaphorical content of the stories or dreams that they experience.

Before becoming a Jungian analyst, Woodman spent many years as a high school teacher of English and Creative Drama. Her love of literature and her direct experience of poetry as a transforming agent in her own life helped her to understand the psychological importance of metaphor. She says, "Being an English teacher, and having had the great privilege of studying and teaching Shakespeare, I accept archetypal images as part of my everyday bread-and-butter world. . . . His characters live in my imagination. His poetry is in my blood."

Her interest in Shakespeare is reflected in the title of her book on eating disorders, *The Owl Was a Baker's Daughter,* which is a line from Hamlet. In her final madness, Ophelia uses this phrase to allude to a medieval Christian tale which would have been familiar to Shakespeare's audience: the baker's daughter, on Christmas Eve, turns away a hungry man, not realizing that he is Christ. Soon, the whole house fills up with the rising dough she refused to share, and the girl herself is turned into an owl. Woodman sees the story as providing a metaphorical context for issues of guilt, greed, spiritual blindness and distorted body image.

"People tend to take even their dreams literally. You dream you have sex with somebody and think, 'Oh, yes, I should go off and have sex with that person.' It's farthest from the truth. The language of dreams is symbolic. The soul world is metaphorical, and if you start acting out everything that comes into your dreams, you just leak the energy and no transformation will take place within the soul. Sexuality *can* have to do with the instincts in dreams, but it can also have to do with the archetype of union, in other words the longing for coming together of the masculine and feminine in the soul."

She feels that metaphor works only when it is allowed to elicit specific and differentiated responses, within the specific and differentiated psyches of individuals. She fears our society's tendency to search out "definitive" but highly restrictive meanings in metaphors, such as many Christians try to impose on the metaphorical parables of Jesus. "The minute you fix it in stone," warns Woodman, "it's gone. It's dead!"

Nevertheless, Woodman feels that metaphor is very much alive in our culture. Though she feels we need to rediscover our responsiveness to the metaphorical value of stories, she sees cultural metaphors emerging in new directions all around us.

"There are new myths: comic books, science fiction, movies. You would think that metaphor was obsolete in the culture until you begin to see it slipping in the back door in so many areas. The human soul is very much in the imagination, and if you take away the food of the soul (metaphor), it'll come slipping in someplace else."

That "someplace else" may be in the renewed attention given to fairy tales by such authorities as Marie-Louise von Franz or Robert Bly. It may be in the symbolic significance of cultural icons like James Dean, Marilyn Monroe, *Gone With the Wind* and *The Wizard of Oz.* Or it may be in the person of storytellers like Marion Woodman, who by virtue of their more "serious" credentials, force us to come to grips, seriously, with the playfulness of metaphor.

6
A Conversation with Marion Woodman*

Cathie: I have heard you refer to patriarchy as being mother-bound. Could you explain that?

Marion: Patriarchy is thought to be synonymous with masculinity, and women tend to blame men for the patriarchy. But women too must take some responsibility for the way things are. It's clear we have suffered in terms of social rights, jobs, abuse and so on. Since early Greek times women have been sacrificed. But there has been a sort of natural, unconscious collusion; men have expected the sacrifice and women have played into the victim role.

In my experience with women in analysis I see how extraordinarily difficult it is for them to emerge from this role. If there's a divorce, for instance, they often want to give some gift to the man. It could be money, the house, the dog—as if they were trying somehow to assuage their guilt at having abandoned the man. It seems to me this is the result of centuries of women catering or pandering to men, and even the most conscious women still get caught.

The fact is that for the most part men are mother-bound boys. Whatever a family may look like from the outside, very often the wife is in fact boss and the man is dependent on her—just as a small boy is dependent on the mother. You see this quite clearly when the woman begins to find her own maturity and stand to her own authentic voice. Then it's the men who fall apart. They aren't able to live their life alone nor have they got the maturity, unless they're working terribly hard on themselves, to be equal to the woman who says, for instance, "I want you to talk to me, I want to know what your feelings are. I want this relationship, I do love you, but I'm not willing to take care of a little boy and I don't want to be mothered by you either."

The archetypal dynamic is that of men pleasing the Great Mother. When men are mother-bound, they don't know what they feel and so they can't act out of their true feelings. They have lived their lives in terms of pleasing Mother. As growing boys their authentic feelings weren't respected or were beaten out of them. As grown men they will do their ut-

---

* Reprinted from *Heartwood,* vol. 7, nos. 3 and 4 (July-October 1988). The interviewers were Cathie Diamond and Susan Riley.

most to please a woman, and that's why it doesn't work. When the woman rebels against being mother, they say, "It doesn't matter what I give her, she wants more." In other words, they see in the woman the archetypal witch who'll take and take and say, "It's not enough."

Cathie: There's a denial in our culture, then, of the power of women?

Marion: Yes, but you see there's an archetype operating here. When a woman is genuinely trying to get out of power—genuinely trying to come from a place of love in herself—the man still tends to project onto her that old mother archetype that wants everything. In the early Great Goddess religions, the supreme sacrifice the man could make was his testicles on the altar of Cybele, which was to sacrifice his manhood to her. Then she was satisfied, and that's what happens in many modern marriages. If a man is hooked into a witch-mother, sooner or later he becomes impotent and then, of course, she becomes furious if he goes off with a younger woman with whom he is not impotent. But it's a double bind, because the reality we are brought up with in our own homes is the only reality we know; if we don't know anything but power we act out of power.

Cathie: Unconsciously?

Marion: Yes, and then we call that power "love" or "loyalty." For me the perfect example of patriarchy—I use "perfect" in a derogatory sense, I mean the worst example—would be the Nazi regime run by little boys—Hitler, Himmler, Göring, Goebbels. Basically, these were mother-bound men, fierce little boys who did everything they could to kill the feminine principle, like setting up breeding farms where they were going to produce the super race. So the patriarchy, from my point of view, is a power-oriented principle where the goal is everything—the perfect product. However, there is no love of the process and everything that doesn't contribute to the perfect product is annihilated. That is against everything the feminine principle stands for.

Cathie: In your books you talk about how women alienated from the feminine principle become male-identified, adopting male values. Is this what you are addressing here?

Marion: In part. What happens in a patriarchy is that the feminine archetype is split, as everything is split in patriarchy—it's an either/or, black and white world. There's no both/and.

Everything becomes dichotomous, so that you have the perfect madonna—chaste, up on a pedestal, pure white. The whole allure of a virgin is that she is perfection. Then on the other side there's the whore, and these two do not come together. That is why in a patriarchal world men tend to have a wife and mother of their children, generally the image of their own mother—*mamma mia*—and hidden away there's a mistress with whom they can experience their lust. In most women's psyches that same split has taken place, so that many women who are trying to come to consciousness are realizing they married their father. The madonna in them chose someone to take care of them, give them security. But as they mature, they are often unsatisfied sexually with such a man, so they look around for someone with whom to experience their harlot.

Women bound into unconscious mother, the same women who look to daddy to take care of them, can go into the flip side and become powerful mother to their little boy in marriage. It's all unconscious. They don't realize that if their role as mother were taken away from them they wouldn't be anybody. That's why so many women go into a terrible depression when their kids leave home. They don't have any identity without somebody to mother.

Cathie: So they are living out the archetype unconsciously and not relating to it?

Marion: They are identified with it. They have no objectivity. The individual woman, the woman inside the role, has not come to consciousness. The woman she was born to be is not there because she is identified with the unconscious side of her own mother—her introjected mother. As you work down deeper, at the heart of the complex is the archetype, the Great Goddess. There's power!

Cathie: When you talk about a woman being penetrated by the masculine, does that mean the woman has to be conscious, she has to be present to be penetrated in this way?

Marion: Yes, and she also has to be very strong as a container—the feminine principle is the container and that's true in a man as well as a woman. Think of a poet like John Donne, for example. He says, "Nor ever chaste except You ravish me," speaking to God, speaking of himself as a poet or an artist. An artist has to be ravished by the archetypal unconscious or there is no art. It's his femininity that is ravished by archetypal energy. So the container has to be strong and at the same time very flexible. It has to be able to stretch to receive the power of the archetype but only while the rapture is on. Then when it's over, the container contracts and the ego takes on its own identity again.

Cathie: And that boundary is clear?

Marion: In true artists it is. They don't imagine their egos created the work of art. It came through them; they were receptive.

When a woman is identified with, rather than related to, the mother archetype, she imagines she knows what's best for her children and she will expect them to perform according to her dictates. That may be all very unconscious and it's never spoken but the child knows it's meant to perform. A woman who is not identified with the archetype knows that there's a far greater power than she that created the child and allowed the child to come into being through her. Then it's her task to create a space in which that child can grow into its own being—be who it was born to be. In other words, she will mirror the child to itself. A woman who's caught up in power is as narcissistic as a man caught up in power. All they can see is themselves. The children are used to mirror the parent and the child may be destroyed.

Many therapists get into this, especially those who haven't had personal analysis. All they can think of is helping—helping their clients or helping their partner, trying to fulfill somebody else's needs, and they have no idea of how to fulfill their own because they themselves have been the children of narcissistic parents.

Cathie: They act out their need—the unconscious mother—but consciously they think they're giving?

Marion: Yes, and they're using the energy from the client. They're telling the client what to do when they have no idea what the client's life is meant to be. But if the client suddenly decides to leave, all hell breaks loose because they are dependent on the client. What the therapist has done has simply recreated what was in the client's home in the first place. And that's tragic for both client and therapist.

In the business world, I hear many women complain about the patriarchal structure they're in, and very often it's a woman who is the worst patriarch. A woman who is driven to perfection can be harder to work for than a man. She can be very cruel to others and just as cruel to herself. I have women working with me who call themselves feminists, trying very hard to find their femininity. They have university jobs or are working toward Ph.D.s where they are forced by the structure to repress the feminine. Because they are on the cutting edge, they are working so hard they are just plain workaholics.

The irony is that they are talking reverently about the feminine and yet they are killing her. They dream of being raped. Their own patriarchal principle is raping their own little girl. Then they break down with candida or some other disease where the immune system turns against them and says, in effect, "You've got to care for your femininity."

Cathie: It seems that a feminist perspective is not always in line with the feminine . . .

Marion: Well, I find it really sad because sometimes I have lectured and I've been talking, as I am now, about women who are trapped in a patriarchal construct. They are not in touch with their own feeling values. They don't know what they, as women, need or want. Then a woman gets up and argues in a strident voice that is not related to her body and becomes the personification of everything I've been talking about. It's just a rant. Her poor body is frightened and shaking. It's not in connection with her head at all. I've tried to dialogue with such women, but they walk out, literally; they won't even relate enough to dialogue the point they've made and they can't receive what I've said.

If there is no trust and no receiving, there is no feminine principle operating. Yes, the terrible irony is that people talk about the feminine principle and they read their notes and talk as fast as they can and all the time the body is wound up in knots. What they are is the very opposite of what is coming out of their lips. They use a feminine language but they've still got the patriarchal way of thinking. I think it is quite clear that the patriarchy is in its last throes, but we are not nearly through it yet.

From a larger perspective, the breakdown of the immune system in the microcosm, the human body, is mirroring what is happening in the macrocosm, the earth. The immune system of the macrocosm is breaking down. It can't help its trees, it can't help its biosphere. And anorexia! So many addictions compensate the extreme of the perfectionist ethic, the opposite of feminine wisdom. The system is breaking down and people can't take it. They say, "If this is what life's about, I'm not interested." Some of them think that blowing up another country is the answer.

We're on the tail end of the patriarchy. What I think is going on is the emergence of the Great Goddess, the feminine side of God. I call her Sophia. I have enough faith in the evolution of consciousness to believe that, just as in their personal life people don't usually bother with the feminine principle unless they are forced to through some illness, so the same thing's happening on the planet—our earth is sick. Fear is going to force us to allow the Goddess in. No, she is forcing her way in whether we like her or not. There has never been feminine consciousness on the planet.

Susan: Never?

Marion: Never. A few individuals, a few of the great saints, certainly knew what femininity was about. In the old matriarchies there was no feminine consciousness, only unconscious mother. The "I"—the ego—with values and truths of its own was not operating. In the Celtic world they died for the Goddess but they had no ego that said, "Life is worth living." They were like the terrorists in Palestine or the I.R.A. who don't have the ego strength to say life is worth living so they willingly die for a cause. Feminine consciousness has been operative in some individuals, but not in a whole culture.

Now I think we're starting to get free of the old matriarchy and free of the patriarchy. In other words, we are entering into conscious relationship with our mother and father complexes. As a planet we're moving toward maturity. We're trying to find out who we are when we're not possessed by those complexes. And we're fighting against time.

In an individual the process is so exciting. You see the feminine, the little girl who's been hiding in the manure pile for forty years, suddenly appear once the old mother and father are out of the way. You see the dreamer go down into the manure pile and scratch away and suddenly there's this little pair of eyes looking up and this tiny, thin creature is quivering in there, and the dreamer says, "What are you doing down there?" and the little girl says, "I would have been killed if I'd come out."

Then it's our task to bring her to maturity and health. You can watch her in the dreams, growing up, going through the initiation rite of puberty. She becomes a conscious virgin who, when she's strong enough, is penetrated by the masculine. It's always a mystery who the lover is—she is suddenly pregnant. In terms of the Christian myth that would be the Holy Spirit. Then that girl will bring forth a glorious boy—a golden boy, a child with wonderful energy.

I think there's a masculinity we have little knowledge of. We've done a lot of work on the feminine, but just as exciting is the masculinity born of that virgin feminine. A woman first has to work through her needs, her feelings and her values. Then the masculine grows up and says, "I will stand up for them; I will put them out there in the world and I will work with you in all your creative activity."

Cathie: Is this the Jungian idea of the positive masculine as help-mate and protector, enabling the woman to set boundaries and discriminate?

Marion: And cut—that's the hard one because sometimes it's the relationship that goes. The man or the woman realizes that the old relationship is not going to work, but there is so much investment in the marriage, the children and the home, that they can hardly bear to make the cut. There's where the masculine has to come in with love and not with power. I think there's a dimension of love that's far beyond what we yet know in terms of healing, in terms of expansion.

You can experience the healing that's going on through the love that exists between two people; you can see the light in the other's body and you can feel it in your own. It's a huge energy.

Susan: And it's light?

Marion: Yes, it's light. When we talk about the feminine, conscious femininity, I think we're talking about light in matter, embodied light, the wisdom of the body, not a dark mass. And, just as in physics matter moves toward light, in the psyche unconsciousness and the darkness of matter is wanting to move toward light. Think of the French Impressionists painting the light in a flower, the light in trees, in an apple, in matter—that's what I call conscious femininity. We come to an awareness of our subtle body in our material body and that's the container strong enough to take the penetration of disembodied light.

Susan: Disembodied light?

Marion: Yes, spirit, pure spirit. If people go into a religious trance disconnected from body, the body starts to shake; they can't control it and they go out of consciousness. Whereas, if they are well grounded in the body, and consciousness of that body is firm, they can receive powerful spiritual light. That's how I image the androgyne—soul (embodied light) receiving spirit. That's where real creativity happens.

Cathie: Would you say the therapeutic process then would be about helping to prepare for creativity?

Marion: For me, that's what it is. And it's not only preparing. It is creating. But all of us have psychic blocks. Sometimes the energy's right there and then the dream will say, "Now look here, something's missing." The bride's all ready; somebody gives her her bouquet but often there's no groom—there's no masculinity ready and strong enough for the feminine. Of course this is mirrored in outer relationships as well.

Then the dream says, "You must cover your forehead. Keep it covered. You are not ready." In other words, keep the spiritual eye covered. That's where the light is going to come in. Then the dreamer often has to enter "the basement under the basement" or a black hole, which is the connection to the base chakra. No marriage can take place because the grounding in the body is not strong enough. A light experience in an ungrounded body can cause psychosis.

The life force radiates from the base chakra—the sheer joy of living: "I'm here and I'm glad I am!" Like a tiny duckling—you see it out there swimming in all the dangers underneath the water and above, as if it were completely safe. Well, a lot of infants don't have that. They've lost it either in the birth process or *in utero*. They know they're not welcome. Take a girl whose parents wanted a boy, there's no way she can be what they want. She can't connect with her body; therefore she lives in the upper chakras, by sheer force of will. She's willed herself to go through school and do everything well and be perfect, thinking that some day she'll find out why others want to live.

When it comes to the crunch they have to face it. Fortunately this point doesn't usually come until very late in analysis, when there's some ego strength. It's truly a shattering experience to realize you don't want to live, and equally shattering to know you do. I think that's one of the problems that can surface in AIDS. An AIDS patient said to me, "I do want to live but I haven't the slightest idea what that means." I've had many anorexics tell me that too. There's the black hole. Archetypally, that's the witch who turns everything to stone.

Cathie: The Medusa?

Marion: Yes, literally you wake up in the morning and you can't get up, and as for doing any work, forget it. There's no interest. Why bother?

Cathie: It must take a lot of drive to live in spite of that.

Marion: Exactly. That's where I see the addiction, in the compulsive drive. It's that drive to try to make ourselves believe that life's worth living, and for God's sake don't fall off the tightrope or we'll drop into the abyss. The abyss is that black hole—it's the chaos that threatens if the rigid structure collapses. If life doesn't take a certain form over which we have control we are terrified. University students may say, "Exams are over, my time isn't structured and I'm wasting it. I don't know what to do. I drink or I do this or that. I'll be glad to go back to school in July." That is really sad. Unless they're doing something to justify their existence they *are* nothing. They can't just celebrate who they are and play.

I love that statement in the Old Testament where Wisdom *plays* around the throne of God. As a child plays, with total concentration. The whole imaginative world lights up. Many people have not experienced that and it's what an awful lot of projection in relationship is about. People get so depressed about the responsibilities and duties of marriage that when they see somebody out there with whom they can play they are fatally attracted. Then when they have to choose, they're heartbroken because they don't want to lose that side of their life and they know they're not going to live it inside their marriage. It really comes down to a conflict between duty and responsibility, and creativity and play. What a hideous decision.

Cathie: What would it take for that to change within a marriage?

Marion: To change the duty and responsibility?

Cathie: Yes.

Marion: Well, both men and women want to play. Picasso played until he died. By play I mean being so closely related to the imagination that you're constantly creating. Every minute is new, spontaneous. That's the feminine principle. Life is never boring because there's always something new happening. Without that we just die. In a marriage each has to say, "Let's figure out how we can play." It doesn't take any money, just a huge leap of faith.

Susan: I bet money comes up as an issue though.

Marion: I'm sure it does. People think they have to take a big trip or expensive lessons in something, because the imagination—that little creature in the manure pile—has been trampled on from the time they were infants. So the imaginative world never blossomed and the energy has to go back to the point at which it was blocked. And it's often an infant that comes out.

People are starving and they're trying to fill the black hole with food. They are trying to fill it with alcohol or drugs or sex. They experience a hole and there *is* a hole, but they can't feed it with concrete. It's got to be with imagination because the soul lives on metaphor. There's the playing again. The soul wants to paint or sing, or write or design buildings, but it must have metaphor because metaphor brings the whole person together. There's where the healing is. We live in a concretized society.

Cathie: And we can kill because we don't have that feeling connection. We can kill the earth and kill each other because there's no feeling.

Marion: It's terrible. The women (I say women because I think they're somewhat ahead, but I know men who are just as far, and when they get into their differentiated feminine they're wonderful), many women dream they have to grieve for their witch. They have killed their husband's feeling without knowing it. The witch is so unfeeling that she damaged her children's souls and her husband's soul, not to mention her own, and now the witch will not grieve. She has no idea what she's done. That's also why people can do what they do to the earth.

Here's where a huge leap of consciousness is going to come in. Some people are saying, "You can't cut down that tree." Then others say, "These people are hysterical; they are dramatic; they are histrionic. We needn't pay any attention to them." Their voices squawk from the top of their head and no resonance comes from their body. It's like listening to a beautiful cardinal with a string around its neck. Without the unity to speak from the cells of our bodies, we cannot empathize with the unity of Earth.

Cathie: What do you mean by "surrender"?

Marion: Many women hate that word. They hear "surrender" and think "yield," "be passive," and they see that as giving way to the male. But the truth is it takes great strength to consciously surrender.

Susan: To the unknown?

Marion: Yes, even in small things. If I surrender to what you're saying, if I take a listening role while you're talking, then I can take in what you are saying. Momentarily I shut up and I receive. But there's tremendous energy in that receiving. I take it down and in and I process it, and then it's your turn to listen while I respond to you. There's a yin/yang balance going on: feminine openness as real energy receives masculine assertion. In love-making surrender is a huge and positive energy.

Susan: When you take it in you can get nourished by it too, but if you're constantly going out . . .

Marion: You set up a barrage.

Susan: Right.

Marion: It all fits together, because if you're frightened of what somebody's going to say to you, you spend so much time trying to figure out how you'll respond that you don't receive. People don't hear each other. They are afraid there's going to be something threatening so they block. Surrendering allows the ego to receive. There's no creativity without being able to surrender. Take dancing, for example. So long as you're doing one, two, three around the floor, dancing is a bloody bore. But the minute you surrender to the music, if you've got a partner who can also surrender, you take off. Watch Baryshnikov. His strong body is the perfect container. A container that cannot surrender is not going to make a great dancer. When the music starts and the spirit comes into that surrendered container, there's the creativity and the real energy and the fun.

Susan: A kind of real power, not controlling power?

Marion: Yes, it's what I call being empowered. Then you're not the slightest bit interested in controlling anybody. You've got so much to do to live your own life that you don't try to control others.

Cathie: I was thinking about Baryshnikov and how he's transformed on stage when that energy comes in. Just literally transformed.

Marion: That's true of any great actor or singer. That wonderful Jessye Norman. She's black, she's immense, and when she sings it's pure energy. It makes you realize that some people are meant to have a big body because there's no way they could contain their energy in a little one.

Cathie: Could you say something about homosexuality? Lesbians feel your books at times exclude their experience.

Marion: I don't mean to exclude them. I just don't like to write outside my own experience. I do, however, have homosexual analysands. In the dream process, they differentiate their masculinity and femininity and work to bring those energies to maturity just as heterosexuals do. In relationship, the masculinity of one meets the femininity of the other and vice versa. Sometimes the energies are the same. There are individual differences, of course.

Cathie: What do you think is the most undermining issue in our culture?

Marion: Confusion between personal and transpersonal energies. Identifying with archetypal energy instead of relating to it and, therefore, failing to live our individual lives. Television and movies and sports—all the projections people put out. They can't tell the difference between an archetypal image and their own life. All these big pop singers carry the projection and kids think, "Oh, if I could just be like that," or "I'm nothing and they're everything." Therapists get this projection too. It's a terrific power game if you play it. Differentiation is essential.

Cathie: A clue to this kind of power dynamic seems to be a vacuous look in the eyes and a powerless sound in the voice—nobody home.

Marion: Nobody home. A hundred years ago Nietzsche said God was dead. It's true. The projection came off of that bearded God in the sky, the Great Father. That energy is no longer in the church for most people. But where did the energy go? People now have no idea what to do with it so they put it on rock stars, on alcohol, on muffins, on healers. In our extraverted society it's all projected out and we're left with the black hole.

Susan: We worship something or somebody.

Marion: Yes, and the individual life is not lived. People will go to great lengths not to hear their inner voices. Even when they're jogging they've got music in their ears. They're terrified of silence because in silence they experience inner nothingness. The imagination's dead or at least dormant. Here we are back to the missing feminine principle. Words like "process" —not interested; "presence"—nobody there; "paradox"—makes no sense. Things are either black or white. "Receiving," "trust," "surrender"—they're just sissy words. All *or* nothing.

Still, if there's nobody home you have to hang on for dear life. It's only when there is presence that you can let go.

Cathie: Could you expand on what you mean by the unlived life?

Marion: It's very sad. In dreams it's the little soul bird—"I only wanted to sing my song." And never sang it. Most people don't even know there was a song to sing. They just don't know.

You see, there's another element in that black hole we haven't talked about. Not only is the life not being lived, but a magnetic, even demonic, pull is luring the ego into unconsciousness. It says, "Why *not* get fatter and fatter and sleepier and sleepier? This consciousness trip is too painful." That's the dark side of the Great Mother. If I identified with that voice, I would soon find myself thinking I was too ugly to live, and then be galvinized into justifying my existence. These extremes leave no room for creative life. Again, all *or* nothing.

The same thing goes on with what I perceive as the Great Father. Without a positive relationship to the masculine archetype, I sit down with my pen and I scratch along and what I write is just crotchety prose. Nothing. But, if I'm not tied up in knots the gift may be given. I may feel the penetration; I can open. It's like intercourse. I do everything I can to prepare my container, and then something else comes through, and I'm writing as if I were on fire. When it leaves I shut my pen down and I'm simply Marion again. We need both sides to really live our lives.

Susan: It's like a ritual, isn't it, around the archetypes?

Marion: Yes, a conscious ritual. Of course, once in awhile they take over. Once in awhile they arrive when we're not prepared. Talk about crossroads! The glory and humility of being human. All *and* nothing.

7

Addiction to Perfection*

Marion Woodman is among a score of Jungian analysts on this continent whose work has burst the bounds of the psychology community and appealed to a much wider audience. Her books address one of the deeper issues of our times: the repression of the feminine principle and its effect on our attitudes toward nature and the physical body.

Her interest in addictions stems from painful personal experience. After struggling with anorexia herself as a young woman, Woodman suffered a near physical breakdown in middle age that forced her to give up her career as a high school English teacher. She went to the C.G. Jung Institute in Zürich, Switzerland, where her dreams guided her on the path to self-healing. "They told me to take the positive metaphors they offered and allow their energy to work in my body," she says, comparing this approach to Carl O. Simonton's, whose work with cancer patients was largely unknown at the time.

Woodman decided while in Zürich to enter training as a Jungian analyst. In 1979 she returned to Canada to practice in Toronto. In the years since, she has specialized in the treatment of addictions. Her work has convinced her that the addict's real search is not for a particular substance, but for meaning in life and food for the hungry soul.

What does it mean to be addicted?

Addicted individuals are being driven by an inner energy toward a particular object—be it alcohol, food, drugs, money or another person. This object is a substitute for something that remains unknown to them; the object is actually the presence of something absent—the presence of an absence. So the more they have, the more they need; the more filled they become, the emptier they feel. Addiction is desire without its true object.

How do you account for this haunting sense of absence?

In both the East and the West, there is a deeply rooted desire or need to transcend who we are. Some higher power, some God, finds us unaccept-

___

* Reprinted from *Yoga Journal,* no. 83 (November-December 1988). The interviewer was Stephan Bodian, editor of *Yoga Journal.*

68

able as we are. We've spent several thousand years learning the arts of self-transcendence. Built into that self-transcendence is a search for the Absolute. We feel ourselves morally obliged to search for this Absolute and to make our lives answerable to it. Heroes in fairy tales, Arthur's Knights of the Round Table, and now space heroes search for it. "May the Force be with you" is their benediction as they lift off to never-never land.

Addictions are based on a longing for presence. Addicts somehow believe they can live in the presence of perfection—perfect body, the perfect man or woman, the perfect nirvana. Addictions aren't just an escape from something intolerable. They're archetypally based on the search for perfection, for the Sun God, for the Holy Grail. Most people believe that any person worth his or her salt will go on this search.

Are there certain disciplines associated with this search?

Yes. Hatha Yoga can be one, especially when it's misunderstood, as it often is in the West. We Westerners tend to forget that people in the East are generally much more rooted in their bodies, and their spiritual disciplines *assume* that rootedness. People who are already in their heads can misuse yoga to take them even farther out of their bodies. I do yoga asanas myself and encourage my analysands to do them, but only with a competent teacher who recognizes the danger of misusing these disciplines to reach a disembodied bliss consciousness free of our limitations. Our limitations are crucial to who we are. They are our friends, not our enemies.

Say a little more about the danger involved.

I'm all for being in harmony with all things, but too often the conditions for that harmony aren't present, and the individual doesn't have the discipline to create the conditions. For example, the junkie on a high may experience himself to be in harmony with all things, but in fact he has no clear perception of the things he claims to be in harmony with. He's merely fantasizing. Likewise, yoga practitioners can go into a fantasy, using yoga to escape reality and leave their bodies behind.

How does this relate to other addictions?

Addictive behavior begins with a yearning to belong—to be a real person in a real situation. But in our society, perfection is confused with reality. Unless you pretend to be perfect, you don't belong; you're considered weird, neurotic or unfit. In the dysfunctional family that pretends to be happy, where food is the center of the family gathering, one child may become a binger, another an anorexic, another a bulimic. The harmony and perfection that everyone pretends is present at the meal is in fact absent, but everyone denies the absence, and the young child, doubting his or her own perceptions, seeks the harmony through food. Denial is fundamental in addictive families: denial of what is not present, the loving family; and denial of what is present, the addiction.

Addicted persons have experienced real trauma. They can't trust reality. The ground of reality—their ability to rely on their own perception of what is real—has been pulled out from under them, and there's a legitimate absence of trust at the core of their being. So they're constantly struggling to approximate or simulate reality, and they can't trust their own simulation either, because it keeps changing. What is ultimately real for them is an absence—an absence of reality. The best they can do is simulate its presence.

In the movie *River's Edge,* Dennis Hopper has a companion, Ella, who is a doll. Hopper knows Ella is a doll, and he turns to her and says, "We know that, don't we, Ella?" In his imagination, her gaping mouth answers, "Yes." The audience can see that Ella is a doll, that one of Hopper's legs is plastic, that the relationship is a parody. Whether they can feel in their bones the tragic commentary on our own society depends on how plastic they themselves are. Many people dream they have plastic limbs or plastic hearts, or that they are dolls or are in love with dolls. They live in simulated bodies in a simulated world. Nothing ultimately exists except what they've invented, and they have to go on inventing because the absence would be overwhelming. The invention, the simulation, is fulfilling real needs; the doll is a substitute for a real companion. But to get rid of the doll means there is no companion at all. How many love affairs do you know that are pure simulation? Still, they're existence itself to the lovers, because the lovers are so needy.

One question that haunts the addict is, "Does anything really exist, apart from my invention of it?" In order to get close to the answer, addicts play Russian roulette with themselves. If I put a bullet into a gun and hold it to my head, I have one chance in six of blowing my brains out. If I die, then my question has been answered—something is real, apart from my invention. If I don't, at least I'm living on the edge. This is the game anorexics, gamblers, alcoholics, fast drivers, are playing. It's also the game our culture, our planet, is playing. How close can we come to the edge without going over?

In the movie *The Deer Hunter,* for example, the thesis was that America was on a high, like an addict, and the Vietnam War was this country's Russian roulette. Americans died, and we discovered that yes, there is a reality out there, the world is not just an American invention. There is grace in that; the fantasy dies. American defeat was grace.

And new life begins.

Yes. Looked at from this point of view, that war was one of the most moving things that happened in the history of America. The soldiers came home maimed. Nobody wanted to see them. The conquering hero image was no more. Then the soldiers who had been through the horror, stoned or not, said, "You have to recognize us; we are your life." In the failure of the conquering hero myth is the possibility of new life for the planet. Recognizing our own failure as conquering heroes, we recognize our own humanness. This is true of the street people, too, the bag ladies, the waifs, the outcasts. In dreams, these are the unknowns who carry the new energy. They don't have the power to say, "Be" and it is. They are part of us, and they are forcing us to realize, culturally and individually, that we must forgo our addiction to omnipotence. To play God is to reject our human reality.

When they finally decided to build a monument in Washington, they had to face this. They couldn't erect statues of soldiers throwing grenades at natives or of soldiers raising the American flag. Such hero imagery is no longer possible; veterans no longer relate to it. Instead, a woman designed a black wall that goes deep into Mother Earth, and on it is inscribed every name of every casualty. Finally America has its Wailing Wall. People come to the wall and feel the names of their loved ones with their fingers, their bodies, and they weep. That's what war is about—tears. And that's what real life is about—suffering, loss, conflict, joy. The dark and the light. What Keats called the "vale of soul-making."

As long as addicts are trying to transcend themselves, reaching for the sky, pulling away from Earth into spirit, they're like some hero carved in stone, standing on top of his pillar alone, blind to the pigeon shit. Instead of transcending ourselves, we need to move *into* ourselves. We're talking about human unsuccess—not failure, but the unsuccess that is human, in contrast to the perfection that rapes the soul.

I'm aware that the word "soul" has a lot of currency these days, especially in Jungian circles. What does it mean, exactly?

"Soul," to me, means "embodied essence," from the Latin verb *esse,* to be. It's part spirit and part matter. Blake says that "body is that portion of soul perceived by the five senses." Through the orifices of our bodies, our souls interact with the outer world. Certainly homemade bread and strawberry jam can feed our soul, and so can Mozart. Soul, I think, has to do with the point where time and the timeless intersect, moments when we experience ourselves and others in our full humanity—part animal, part divine. Traditionally, soul is thought of as feminine, as matter is thought of as feminine. So long as we are on this Earth, body and soul are inextricably bound together. Neither is perfect by absolute standards. When that perfectionist ideal starts calling out the orders and laying down the judgments, some delicate feminine creature is raped in our dreams.

Why do you think addiction is so prevalent in our times?

Technology is driving us faster and faster, and it more and more obliterates the individual soul. Centuries of patriarchy and patriarchal values have put the emphasis on goals, achievement, competition, product. Now, of course, we're starting to reject those values, because we're finding that life isn't worth living if we're always running as fast as we can. My therapy practice is largely made up of people who have finally said, "If this is life, I don't want to live."

Yes, but achievement and productivity are the ideal in our culture. The addict is just an intensified example of a way of being that most of us, in one way or another, have adopted.

Yes. And it has been passed down to us by our parents and our grandparents. Our parents had standards for us, they expected a certain performance, and we tried to live up to their expectations. But when this happens, children learn to perform rather than to be who they are, and the soul goes into hiding—in a manure pile in dreams, for example. As adults, they never think about their own reactions. Instead they wonder, "Who should I please here in order to make the best performance?" After you've pleased mother and father and teacher and husband and boss, you finally get to the point where you start asking, "Who am I?" and "What are my needs?" This is the point where many people recognize that they are on a suicidal journey. Their perfectionist ideals have lured them away from their own life. The underlying question becomes, "Do I want to live?"

Some addicts decide that if this is what the world is, they don't want any part of it. Others say, "Yes, I'd like to live, but I have no idea what that means." They are so out of touch with the life force, the sheer joy of being alive. I think most people rarely experience this joy, and, as a result, they are living by will power. Eventually will power breaks down, and it's a good thing it does, because then there's a chance for self-cure.

You see, I look at neurosis creatively, as Jung did. A neurosis or an addiction will not allow a person to go on living an empty non-life. Unless the person chooses to be blindly unconscious, eventually he or she asks, "What is this compulsion that is destroying me?" and, even more important, "Who am I?"

So there's a wisdom in the addiction, ultimately.

Yes, if the person takes the time to find it. I really like working with addicts, because they're desperate, and they have fierce energy. Their dreams are full of wolves, and mythologically the wolf is the animal of Apollo, the sun god and also the god of creativity. These wolves represent a ferocious hunger for something; the addict doesn't know what it is. From a Jungian perspective, the psyche naturally moves toward wholeness. If we become stuck in a way of life that is not right for us, or a psychological attitude that we've outgrown, then symptoms appear that force us out of our nest, if we're willing to deal with them. If we choose not to, then we become obsessed with something that concretizes a genuine spiritual need.

Jung, for example, worked with one of the founders of AA. "The craving for alcohol," he wrote, "is the equivalent, on a low level, of the spiritual thirst of our being for wholeness; expressed in medieval language: the union with God." Alcohol, he pointed out, is *spiritus* in Latin. If that wolf energy can be lovingly disciplined and turned in the right direction, it can be powerfully healing and creative. That's what the addict's journey is all about—it's a spiritual search that's become perverted. You see it in the rituals that addicts engage in. If you work with these rituals creatively, you will often find profound religious activity going on there.

Give an example of a ritual that an addict might perform.

Well, real bingers will not tell anybody what they're going to do on Friday night, but they will plan very carefully the food they're going to eat. Usually it includes something sweet, something made with milk, and something made with grain. These are exactly the foods used in the ancient goddess rituals. Often they'll wear a particular ritual outfit; they'll disconnect the telephone, lock themselves in their room, and begin eating, consciously at first. But at the point where instinct can no longer be disciplined, they lose consciousness and start wolfing food down. They don't taste it; they don't want it; they want oblivion.

You see, there's tremendous excitement before the binge begins, tremendous anticipation that they're about to move out of the unbearable two-dimensional world and into the presence of divine sweetness and nourishment. Metaphorically, this is the divine Mother. In sacred ritual, the ego crosses into sacred space and surrenders to the divine. That's the whole point. When the god enters, the ego opens and expands, and although it returns to profane space when the ritual is over, it has touched into a timeless world that gives meaning to this one. Consciousness is the key.

Addicts' rituals focus on a concrete god—alcohol, gambling, hedonism—that annihilates their ego and drives them into meaningless unconsciousness. When they wake up, they feel duped. Instead of being connected to a richer meaning in their life, they are further alienated and alone. Their self-esteem plummets, and they drop into the suicidal fantasies so characteristic of addicts. Their basic impulse is a natural one to find another dimension—but they have the wrong god. For most people the Judeo-Christian tradition no longer holds the numinosity, the light, the consciousness that enriches the soul. So they're trying to find it in their own living room.

You talk in several of your books about the relationship to the mother and about mothering that fails to contain and hold the infant in a loving way. How does that contribute to addiction?

Enormously. A mother who doesn't love her own body is not connected to her own life energy. She cannot mirror her child in its own Beingness, and therefore cannot connect the child to its own feelings in its own body. The child doesn't develop a strong container with firm boundaries. Ultimately it's cut off from its own inner life. Mother is "mater," and few of us love our own matter.

And this love of our own matter is transmitted from the mother?

Yes. But very few mothers have it in our culture, because they didn't receive it from their mothers. Many women feel tremendous guilt about their mothering, but they can't give what they weren't given unless they work on themselves. Look at the treatment of the feminine principle in our culture. People say they care, yet they rape Mother Earth at such a pace that we could end up destroying ourselves in blind stupidity.

In that sense, the entire socioeconomic system is involved in a kind of addiction. We're destroying ourselves in a binge of consumption.

Yes. Mired in matter, concretized *mater* (mother), which compensates for the patriarchal demand for perfection. The more we try to transcend ourselves, the more we are unconsciously trapped in our own materialism. Microcosm and macrocosm mirror each other. Just as we rape our own bodies, we rape our Earth. We put cement over her, we destroy her rain forests, her ozone layer. Meanwhile both men and women dream incessantly of being raped. What does that mean metaphorically? It means that our feminine body/soul is being ravaged by a power principle that doesn't care one bit what happens to us as human beings. The feminine soul that would move with the majestic rhythms of nature into creative, whole living is considered slow, stupid and irrational.

In some way, then, mothers have to affirm a love of life in order to transmit this love to their children.

But they can't if they have no idea there's anything to life but performance. One of my clients told me a story about how he came home from school very late once as a small boy because he had stopped by the river and found some beautiful little stones. He had filled his pockets with them and come running home to give them to his mother. She was furious with him and turned him upside down and shook him, and the stones went all over. "Now pick them up," she told him, "and throw them out in the lane where they belong." Well, that was traumatic for him, because he truly loved those stones. They had a numinosity for him, and his mother had no sense at all that he was offering his soul to her. She rejected his beingness. No mother would do that purposely, I would hope. But if she doesn't have that inner sense she focuses on his disobedience instead of his soul.

So there's no one to blame. It's just that this is what has been transmitted from generation to generation.

It's the world we're living in. And it's our responsibility to become conscious and stop it. The feminine is rumbling with rage and grief. The frenzied addict eventually has to look her in the eye. And so does our frenzied world. We have to discover the magnificent consciousness in matter, and in our own bodies. We are capable of seeing the light in a rose bush, of feeling the energy in a tree. We are born to live in the love that permeates all life.

What is the alternative for your analysands who have addictive problems? How can they heal themselves from this negative addictive spiral?

It's a long, hard struggle, because the reality we are raised in is the only reality we know. We act toward ourselves and others as we were acted upon. If the authority figures in our childhood acted out of power, demanding the best little boy or girl, the best little scholar, the best little athlete, the child introjects that power and constantly criticizes, evaluates and judges himself or herself. An inner voice is constantly saying, "Who I am is not lovable. I must do something special in order to deserve love. I'm not good enough, I should be better, I should be able to make a faster decision, I should have more courage, I should, I ought to, I have to." A person can learn to recognize that voice and separate it from his or her essence, can learn to say, "That's not me saying that, it's my unconscious parent blathering inside my head. I can concentrate on hearing my own voice, my own needs, my own feelings." That's when healing begins.

First of all, though, it seems you'd need enough perspective to be able to see the part that's tormenting you, as well as a willingness or desire to disidentify from it. Otherwise there must be a very strong tendency to get sucked right back into it, to say, "Okay, you're right, I totally agree with you, I'm a worthless piece of shit."

Exactly. That's the old pattern, and I don't know any way out of it if you don't have a creative outlet. You have to find your own way of expressing who you are. If it is your way, you won't inflate it.

You can't face that compulsive part of you head on ?

 You can, but you'll lose. It's an evil energy that wants to rob us of our life. Facing it directly constellates its negative power.

So we need to use soul-making to strengthen our own soul, and let that be a kind of shield or protection against the evil.

If you promise to limit yourself to 500 calories a day, or to quit smoking or drinking, all you do is strengthen the unconscious, which says, "No, I'm not going to do what you say." You set up a series of polarities that can't possibly be resolved—everything is either all black or all white, you're either completely sober or you're out of control—and you're swung back and forth between these two poles. It's a very patriarchal way of seeing things. It leads to despair, which is negative inflation.

It's literally a set-up, because pretty soon the unconscious will overcome the ego, and your will power will be destroyed.

Yes, and if you've lived with an addiction all your life, you have a very weak ego to begin with. As I see it, the feminine way is the healing way. Rather than polarizing, the feminine accepts the paradox: this is beautiful, *that* is the opposite, but it too is beautiful. Our culture says thin is beautiful, but that doesn't mean fat people are ugly. In fact, many people are diminished when they lose weight. Every body has its right size for the amount of energy it contains. The problem is to keep the energy flowing instead of blocking it in fat.

In some way, then, the body has a wisdom such that, if left to itself, it will choose its natural size.

And the body also has a wisdom such that it recognizes when the soul is so frightened, and so unable to cope with the world, that it has to have some kind of soporific. The food or the alcohol or the drugs are keeping the pain down or keeping the fear away. Or excess body weight may act as armor to protect the soul. Women, for example, who quickly lose a hundred pounds may suddenly find themselves attractive to men. If they haven't developed psychically, they are like five-year-olds in a mature body. The child can't deal with the sexuality, so the body takes on weight again for protection. Or it breaks out in a rash, or vaginitis, or some other symptom. The truth is, the body is the best friend we have, although most of us think it's our worst enemy. It's like a donkey that gets beaten again and again, but it still tries to hold whatever balance it can.

When you talk about trying to subdue the addiction through will power, I think of the first of the Twelve Steps of AA, which says that we admitted we were powerless over our life, and that through will power alone we couldn't do anything about it.

Right. There's the addict, who wants control above all else, having to admit to being powerless. But it's the first step.

I have immense respect for AA. Many of the addicts I'm working with are in Alcoholics Anonymous or Overeaters Anonymous. And the Twelve Steps are the natural progression that emerges in dreams. Where I think my work complements AA is in its emphasis on creativity and the feminine mode—the soul-making we talked of earlier. You sit down and listen to your own body. You reflect on your day; you write, you paint, you put your soul down on paper or into your music or your dancing or your sculpting, whatever your creative outlets may be. You become so interested in nourishing and releasing the inner being that you're not driven to the refrigerator or the liquor cabinet. Of course, it can take immense discipline to say, "Stop it."

What about the importance of imagination in the soul-making process?

Soul work is an act of the imagination. The soul lives on metaphor. For example, you've seen great athletes stand still and imagine themselves doing a dive or clearing the high bar, then go into the actual dive or jump. If they can't see themselves completing it, they know they won't be able to. Addicts suffer from failure of the imagination. They become imprisoned in rigid attitudes. They can't imagine freedom, and because they deny reality they can't change it. They fail to make the necessary rites of passage from one stage of life to another, fail to mature, fail to get out of boring jobs or destructive relationships. They fail to see the meaning of what they are living. Their dreams would tell them, if they would pay attention. The metaphors in dreams give us a picture of our psychic condition and how to change it.

So through metaphor the body talks to the spirit and the spirit talks to the body. I notice you use the word "metaphor" and not "symbol."

They are basically the same thing. I like the word "metaphor" because it comes from the Greek for "transformer." And that's exactly what a metaphor is: it transforms one kind of energy into another. Soul work is incarnation, the process of spirit incarnating in the body. The soul is in the body for however long we live and has its work to do while we are here. But many people just obliterate soul. They go as fast as they can at their work or some other addictive behavior, and the soul becomes more and more frenzied. As the soul becomes more frenzied, so does the body, because the soul lives in the body.

So we are filling up our lives with material things, with doing and accomplishing, and not heeding the soul's need for metaphor—for aesthetic experience, poetry, being in nature, silence, writing and so forth.

Yes. Anything creative. If you give yourself half an hour a day with your dreams or your music—whatever your creative process—the soul becomes very quiet. You're located in your body, and you feel nourished by the activity. Addiction, in contrast, thrives on frenzy. The faster the person goes, the greater the frenzy, whereas to become quiet and live with these metaphors is to go back to your own creating.

Much of my work with addicts centers on trying to find the metaphor that the addictive object represents for them and then encouraging them to bring that metaphor to consciousness. Alcohol, for example, represents the spirit that the addict longs for. Food, I think, is very often the positive mother, the one the addict didn't have.

The same with compulsive relationships, where there is a longing for wholeness through union with another person—the other person carries the projection of that totality in concrete form. In working with metaphor, I try to take a powerful image from the dream and have the person concentrate on it, meditate on it, perceive it, reflect on it. Meditation on the metaphor objectifies the energy and thus transforms it. Particularly with psychosomatic problems, metaphor is often a very powerful healer. By imagining the metaphor in the body and concentrating on it, new energy is released. Matter and spirit cooperate in the healing process.

An anorexic, for example, may dream there's going to be a wedding, but the wedding can't take place until some work is done. She doesn't know what the work is, but until it's done, the spiritual eye must remain veiled, the forehead shielded. Then she's told she has to go down and clean up the garbage in the basement. Sometimes there's a cat lost in the furnace pipes, or a little girl buried underneath a pile of manure, and she's starving, she has huge eyes, and she looks into the dreamer's eyes and says, "You're trying to kill me." In other words, before the dreamer can continue on her spiritual search, she has to clean up the garbage in her basement, at the deepest levels in her body, the deepest levels of soul. She has to come to terms with the starving child inside.

Very often there's a huge snake down there as well, which represents kundalini, and the dreamer is awestruck by this incredible serpent power. A connection has to be made at the deepest body level before the inner marriage can take place. It is very dangerous if we try to fly into spirit before we're grounded in the body. Too much light too fast, and we're blown away. That's what happens to genuine anorexics. They hate their filthy bodies. They want so much spirit, so much light, that they'll starve themselves into euphoria and then run and hyperventilate in order to get it. But they're being carried off the earth, and they've vacated their body.

And that's why creativity can be so healing. Because in order to be creative, in order to engage in soul-making, you have to listen to your body.

Exactly. True creativity, true soul-making, comes from that deep communication with what Jung would call the archetypal world. That's where the real nourishment is. But to be in the body also means to suffer; that's why most addicts are trying to avoid it. Suffering is ultimately healing.

Say a little more about that.

Well, I think the word "love" is just bandied around in our culture. To me, real love, the move from power to love, involves immense suffering. Any creative work comes from that level, where we share our suffering, just the sheer suffering of being human. And that's where the real love is.

Compassion, of course, means "to suffer with."

Yes. But not at a superficial level. Addicts are so busy trying to find something on the surface that they never take the time to drop into process where the real healing happens. They never stop long enough to allow presence, to be in the present. They live either in a fantasized paradise that is past or in a fantasized glorious future. They lock themselves into one rigid way of behaving in an attempt to get control of their lives, all the time terrified that they'll lose control, and denying the fact that they already have. "If only I could lose weight, if only he loved me, if only I could stop drinking, if only . . ." is the cry that silently breaks their heart. Real imagination is at work when one day the addict can say, "I am. I am loved. I can receive love. I do love myself. I do love."

I remember when that realization struck me. It was as if Niagara Falls had broken open my heart, and I was a frail atom in the universe with some incredible energy pounding through me. That night I dreamed of a tidal wave relentlessly pushing its way. On its crest was an immense chocolate-colored woman, her magnificent arm upraised like Delacroix's *Liberty.* She was moving in and nothing could stop her. Then I was a molecule in the wave, in harmony with countless other molecules. We were all empowered with the love that would bring her to land.

That's where I think the healing is. We're being forced out of our tiny individual, cultural and national boxes, and we're beginning to dream of an embodied consciousness, a global harmony that resonates through everything. That's the real bridge between disembodied spirit and unconscious matter.

Could you elaborate?

Well, as I see it, we're all addicts, because we experience ourselves as emptiness swinging in empty space between spirit and matter. Located nowhere. Someone, something out there must have the answer. The more our spirit attempts to escape from this impossible world by transcendence or theorizing (fantasizing or fanaticism), the more our animal body compensates by becoming a garbage disposal, consuming everything we stuff into it. We're the children of a creator, yes, but we're also the children of a creatrix. Until we know her through the metaphors born of our own sacred matter, we're trapped in our own void. The healing power lies in the metaphor. The creative imagination binds together the physical and spiritual, all that is spirit being pictured in the flesh. When Matisse was asked whether he believed in God, his response was, "Yes, when I'm working."

8

The Conscious Feminine*

The feminine in many guises—like the Black Madonna and the Crone—is erupting in individuals the world over. What better spokesperson to announce Her coming and share Her wisdom than Marion Woodman.

Common Boundary: What are you currently thinking about? What excites you?

Marion Woodman: Right now, I'm interested in a new consciousness that is manifesting in dreams. It has not yet reached the conscious level in the everyday world, but people who are in relationship to their dreams are contacting something that's quite new. It's coming through in metaphor, in images.

CB: What kind of images and metaphors?

MW: The Black Madonna, for example. Sometimes she's crying. Sometimes she's austere. She's dark. Sometimes she's a black woman or Indian or Portuguese. I think she's dark because she's unknown to consciousness. She often has a fierce sense of humor that cuts straight through the madness of human behavior. She's always larger than life, which suggests she's a goddess, fit to be the mother of a god.

Throughout history, the Black Madonna has presided over fertility, sexuality and childbirth. She is nature impregnated by spirit, accepting her own body as the chalice of the spirit. She has to do with the sacredness of matter; the intersection of sexuality and spirituality. Rejected by the patriarchy, her energy has been smoldering. It is now erupting in individuals and in the planet, demanding *conscious* recognition. Integrating what she symbolizes involves the redemption of matter.

Sometimes she has a son with her. He, too, is an outcast—outcast by the power principle that can only destroy our global village. Her son is an image of potential masculinity, which is very different from what we generally associate with patriarchy. We tend to confuse the patriarchal power

* Reprinted from *Common Boundary*, vol. 7, no. 2 (March/April 1989). The interview was conducted by Barbara Goodrich-Dunn, a counselor in Washington, DC, specializing in body-centered psychotherapy.

principle, which controls and shapes nature at any cost, with masculinity. If we ever bring the Black Madonna's son to consciousness, our idea of mature masculinity will be revolutionized.

CB: Does the Black Madonna arise in the dreams of men as well?

MW: Yes, she appears in the dreams of men and women who are reflecting on their inner world.

The Black Madonna usually appears outdoors, so she's related to nature. My sense is that she has to do with consciousness in matter. We cannot go back to identifying with *mater,* unconscious matter; and there never has been an era of conscious femininity The world has never known Conscious Mother; let alone Conscious Mature Woman. We have to connect to her because the power that drives the patriarchy, the power that is raping the earth, the power drive behind addictions, has to be transformed. There has to be a counterbalance to all that frenzy, annihilation, ambition, competition and materialism.

The Black Madonna is the bridge. She is a spiritual figure in a physical body, so she acts as a bridge between head and heart. She's a wisdom figure. In the Tarot pack, for example, Wisdom is always pictured with a rainbow and irises. The rainbow is a symbol of the connection between heaven and earth. Iris, who in mythology is also a wisdom figure, goddess of the rainbow, is the bridge. I see the Black Madonna as a wisdom figure. Sophia means wisdom, the deep feminine wisdom that manifests through nature, including human nature. Sophia's first appearance in dreams is often as a dark goddess.

CB: How do you envision conscious femininity manifesting itself?

MW: Let's begin with conscious mothering, which is very different from unconscious mothering. A conscious mother is not identified with being a mother. An unconscious mother finds her meaning, her whole identity, in mothering. Very often it ends up that she imposes power on her children. A mother who is identified with being mother has to have children who will eat what she gives them to eat and do what she wants them to do. They remain children in relation to her mothering.

CB: So there's a will to create a form and image, impose it on the body and on the spirit, and eliminate all in the child that does not fit the image.

MW: Yes, unconsciously to do that. This kind of mothering would supposedly be done out of love. When there's a full breast, somebody has to drink from it. It becomes an unconscious drive, and of course it's not all negative.

When I go to our summer retreat, for example, I drop into the Mother. I surrender to nature for a couple of weeks. I choose to do that and it's wonderful. I don't know what time of day it is. I have no sense of a rational, organized frame. I eat and sleep when I want. I allow myself to dream in the loving arms of the Great Mother.

CB: You experience diffusion.

MW: Yes, total letting go. Nature is her gift. I swim, watch the stars, love the trees, feel the energy of the hot rocks, feed on the fruits of Mother Earth. It's beautiful. But it's totally unconscious.

CB: There's no will involved.

MW: None! I don't even care what day it is. I generally live a very disciplined life, but I think it's necessary once in a while to break away from that. Usually, I get rather bored after about two weeks. I want to come back to consciousness.

Conscious femininity, you see, is not just a blissed-out state. It involves an awareness of the energy of the rock and the love in the bird, the tree, the sunset. An awareness of the harmony of all things, an awareness of living in the world soul. The intuition, the attunement of the body is concentrated, alive. The capacity to be open and to receive is an alert state. You feel the harmony of the whole universe in the marrow of your bones.

CB: So you experience pleasure, but not the oblivious pleasure of addiction that you write about. In addictive pleasure, one is absent, unconscious.

MW: In addictive oblivion, no ego is present to bring the experience back into consciousness. So, however high the addict flies, the treasure is lost because there's no ground to bring it home to. It's an escape from reality. In the experience I am describing the ego surrenders to another reality, but it is a conscious receiver. It can bring the treasure back to consciousness and life is enhanced. I don't pretend to understand the mystery, but I do experience something awesome going on between me and other living things: a bone-deep unity and wholeness. And consciousness grows as a result. In the addictive state, consciousness doesn't grow. Once in a while you get creative seeds in the oblivious state, but they don't stay unless you nourish them—paint, dance, write. Whatever state of oblivion I am in, I try to dance and write every day.

CB: Doesn't that pull you out of your diffusion?

MW: No, I let my body become the music and do what it wants to do. Or

I let my pen go for a walk in that twilight zone between consciousness and the unconscious. It finds images and ideas that my ego never finds.

CB: It sounds like you are not organizing, figuring or analyzing.

MW: No, not at all. At times, I dance or write—from the sheer need to express joy, anguish or rage.

CB: Why do you think we are afraid of that diffusion?

MW: I think we're afraid of it because we use so much energy trying to control our lives, trying to keep ourselves disciplined, staying with clocks and calendars. It takes immense energy to keep the worlds we're trying to control going. We put ourselves into controlled little boxes where we are king or queen, where we are omnipotent as long as we can keep our boxes small enough. But smashing against those frail structures is the chaos of the unconscious which is ready to bombard us like Niagara Falls. If we have any consciousness at all, we know that. We know our boxes are shaking. Sometimes people get that shaking in their dreams and nightmares.

On the broader level, there's danger to the planet. Many people are dreaming about earthquakes, nuclear war, the extinction of animal species. People are unconsciously afraid. Those dreams are terrible dreams. There's an immense fear of chaos bursting out. People are afraid of possession.

CB: By the archetypes?

MW: Yes, and for good reason. Their egos are not strong enough to deal with the power of the archetypes. They become possessed. That's what unconsciousness is. Take the mother I spoke of earlier. If you are possessed by the mother archetype, you are just "mother." No ego says, "You are something besides a mother." No ego says, "I want to take responsibility for my own life, not put it on my children." People do very strange things when they are possessed by an archetype. Women, for example, can become possessed by the archetype of victim or martyr and live it out. It is dangerous. There is good reason to be afraid of that diffusion.

CB: You work primarily in Canada, and although Americans tend to lump Canada and the United States together they are quite different psychologically. Do you see the conscious feminine beginning to emerge in the U.S.?

MW: I think it's all over the world. Certainly, Americans are dreaming about the Black Madonna. Remember a woman designed the Vietnam War Memorial. It's low to the ground, it's black. You can put your fingers on those names and reflect, and depart from the wall sadder and wiser. There's soul-making there. It's a completely different concept from the traditional phallic, heroic monuments soaring into spirit. One reason I wanted to come to Washington was to see that monument. I've seen it on television. I've seen the incredible effect it has on people, the weeping and the soul-searching. It must have something to do with being able to touch those names, to be close and feel, soul touching soul through the sacred matter of the monument. I see the Vietnam Memorial as a Black Madonna who holds in her arms all the Vietnam dead, takes them into her warm earth, her conscious matter.

CB: If the Black Madonna is coming, and I've certainly heard this from others . . .

MW: She's coming through dreams. Dreams are ahead of consciousness.

CB: If this energetic force is coming, what will struggle with it?

MW: Patriarchy. Patriarchy is not going to give up easily. Technology is not going to give up easily. I'm not talking about wiping out patriarchal and mechanistic modes of being, but there has to be a balance. Take toxic waste, for example. On the one hand, we give the Third World money to eat and we talk about a global village, about harmony and love. Then we dump our toxic wastes that kill their farms. They ask a paltry $100 to take a barrel of toxic waste. It's the same with acid rain. The factories that are making money are also making acid rain. They are not going to voluntarily shut down. The cedars die and the lakes become polluted, but finance and politics ignore the fact that when a species is extinct, it's finished. It costs more to deal with the garbage than to dump it in the lake. So we dump it in the lake!

CB: You've spoken about how Jungians are frequently accused of narcissistic self-absorption, that all psychotherapy is. But it sounds like what you're seeing in dreams is an incoming energy that challenges the idea that psychotherapy and dream work is only selfish navel-gazing. The personal work people do brings forth that larger energy—the soul.

MW: Rather than "brings forth," I would say "resonates with." Abandoned souls have a way of bringing themselves forth, whether we work on ourselves or not. They are starving, crying out for spirit, crying out for union with the divine. We confine them to prison when we concretize their agony. We try to satisfy their divine yearning with food, alcohol, sexual union. Their cravings seem insatiable because we fail to understand their language. When we connect with our souls, we connect with the soul of every human being. We resonate with all living things. That's where I think the healing is. The Vietnam Memorial is a healing metaphor.

CB: You're talking about the World Soul, not just an individual psychological phenomenon?

MW: Yes, I am. I think there's a point where psychology becomes a spiritual journey. You have to rebuild rotten foundations, deal with the negative mother and negative father. But once the depths are reconstructed, you can't go on wallowing in negativity. That's not only boring, it's destructive. There's a point, I think, where grace enters. It brings with it a whole new concept of love.

CB: How do you see the conscious feminine evolving?

MW: Out of the conscious mother, conscious matter, comes the Virgin. That's the stage many of us are floundering in now, the mature feminine symbolized by the Virgin. I say feminine and not female because this is happening to men also. The Virgin is who she is because she is living her own essence. The Latin verb *esse* means to be, present tense, I am. She is aware of her own feelings, needs and values, and has the courage to act on them. She has presence. She's much more interested in process than results. She understands resonance—truth resonating in her body, like an echo chamber saying, "Yes." She's a receiver.

Any artist, male or female, has to open that receiver, that womb, as wide as possible to let new life penetrate from the unconscious. I think we're going through a revolution as we try to find our real values. It's causing intense problems in relationships.

CB: Are women leading the way in this?

MW: Yes, in relationships for the most part. I think a lot of men are shocked when they see that women have really changed. They think we've been just scribbling in our journals.

CB: That's trivializing.

MW: Of course. They think we're sentimental little girls who've been writing in our little books the way stereotyped Victorian women wrote in their little books—in a naive and uninitiated way. Suddenly, when a woman says, "Look, this is what I think," her man can't believe what's coming out of her mouth. Often it takes a real crisis, she has to threaten to leave to get him to hear her. The projection he has on her as his beloved who'll be exactly as he wants her to be comes from the mother complex. Mother will put up with anything. Mother is unconditional love. When a woman says, "You must see me as I am," she is no longer his ideal woman. But if his lifeline is to his mother-wife, he can't bear to hear that. His umbilical cord is being cut.

Women are tending to take the lead, but there are men taking the lead as well. There are many women whose glass houses with their daddy-husbands are being shattered. I think women are biologically closer to their bodies than men because they come into contact with repressed rage, fear and grief more quickly. Men are just beginning to touch theirs, but the anguish in their bodies is just as terrible.

I want to say one other thing about the feminine because the feminine always comes in threes: mythologically there are the three graces, the three Norns, the three wyrd sisters. We have talked about Mother and Virgin. The third is the Crone, the woman who has gone through her crossroads. Hecate, the goddess of the crossroads, is the Crone. The crossroads in Europe still have little cairns where people drop their stones in honor of the goddess. Those cairns have always been the places of Hecate. The crossroads represents a place where consciousness is crossed by the unconscious—in other words, a place where you have to surrender your ego will to a higher will. The Crone has gone though one crossroads after another. She has reached a place of surrender where her ego demands are no longer relevant. This is the positive side of the Crone. She is a surrendered instrument and therefore detached.

Detachment doesn't mean indifference. It means she has been there. She has suffered, but she can draw back from the suffering. A conscious person in the presence of an unconscious person's pain may suffer more than the unconscious person. So, it's not that she doesn't suffer. It's not that she's indifferent or withdrawn. She's right there, totally present. She's got nothing to lose. She can be who she is and live with the straight, flat-out, naked truth. Therefore the Crone acts as a tuning fork in an environment because she is so real herself. She rings a true tone. People are brought into harmony with that tuning, so it's very releasing. People can respond to their own true tone. The Crone can afford to be honest. She's not playing games anymore. She brings people into that soul space where all outer conflicts dissolve and they can experience their own essence.

CB: As I listen to this, I imagine a journey to that stage involves an enormous amount of sacrifice. I think it's risky to go to that stage.

MW: It is risky.

CB: Usually, when we think of the Crone, she has a negative image—unlovable, for example . . .

MW: The silly old woman at the end of town, the hag . . .

CB: The crazy lady.

MW: Of course, in a selfish narcissistic society this kind of femininity does look crazy, unless you're in real trouble and you want somebody who understands and who is empathic and has no desire for power. She has nothing to lose. Who she is cannot be taken away from her. She has no investment in ego. Therefore, there is no power operating. She's the kind of person you can honestly talk to, profoundly trust. She has no reason to persuade you to do anything or be anything other than who you are.

She's a perfect mirror for a person. You talk to her and she'll mirror you right back. I don't mean to idealize her. I know there is a negative side to the Crone, but your own tuning fork will tell you whether she's lived through her own crossroads. If she hasn't, don't trust her. She'll be into power. Another quality of a mature Crone is a developed masculinity.

CB: In what sense?

MW: I would think of her masculinity as being very discerning, with no sentimentality. She would be able to cut with a well-honed sword. She would be able to see what is no longer essential to life—a relationship, for example, that has become destructive. She would perceive it, see through to the heart of it, and cut where necessary, but cut with love. I always envision her wielding a golden sword with a silver handle. All the perceptivity of gold, but handled with the love of silver. The masculine and feminine together. She has the kind of wisdom that takes life with a grain of salt, smiles at the divine comedy.

I have known four or five Crones, two of them men. I have gone to them when I thought I couldn't go any further. Their love was palpable. No advice. Simply being, saying almost nothing. I knew I was totally seen and totally understood. They could constellate my own inner healer because they could see me as I am.

CB: The condition of the Crone is truthfulness. The fact that there are no illusions creates a container. You can be naked. This is healing.

MW: Exactly. When you are naked, the truth sets you free no matter how awful it is. She's willing to be naked, too. Now we come back to the Black Madonna. Real love happens when embodied soul meets embodied soul. Not in spirit, not in that disembodied world where we want to be perfect, but in life, when we're changing the diapers of someone we love who is dying of cancer, swabbing their lips, when we're doing things we didn't think we could do, when we're stripped of all pride. Our friend is stripped;

we are stripped. There is no false modesty. We are stripped of everything that is unreal and the two of us are there together. I can't even put it into words. Where soul meets soul, that's love.

It hasn't got anything to do with what generally passes for love in our culture. That's just neurotic need. This other is a power that comes through a finely tuned instrument, a container strong enough to receive it. It opens your heart. A real Crone can bring you into touch with that.

I knew an old man, a fabulous Crone, who saved my life. E.A. Bennet, whom I write about in my books, was an eighty-year-old analyst. He could put me in touch with my feelings when I, who was so smart and rational, couldn't feel anything. He would just sit there and feel for me until I got the message. Tears would start to run down my face, not because I was sad, but because I recognized myself. I was picking up my own feeling from him. Then I realized what I really do value. He could perceive the feeling values I had lost touch with.

I think such people will be incredibly important in the future. It's unbelievable how old people are treated in our culture, how people who have been honored all their lives are thrown out into the dust pile. In so many tiny ways, feeling is just tossed aside. How to recapture it without being with someone who can feel, I don't know. A heart attack, a kidney breakdown perhaps . . .

CB: You're very serious about this.

MW: I'm not an evangelist, but I work every day with anguish that is almost unbearable. When I realize what the human soul suffers and with what courage and strength people are silently living, I just stand in awe of what they are going through. And no one knows. It's a profound honor and responsibility to share life at that level and I honor the sharing. I guess you could say I wouldn't be sitting here if I hadn't taken this seriously. I was quite ill, knocked down. I either had to take it seriously or die. I still do. I also feel equally strongly about the earth.

When I picture this vulnerable little ball turning in the universe and I study the thrust of the dreams people bring me, I'm convinced that consciousness is trying to move from power to love. If we're going to be a global village, members of that larger community, receiving each other with all our differences, we need to accept ourselves as imperfect human beings. That involves a whole new understanding of what love is.

CB: The images of love through the media . . .

MW: Sentimental crap.

CB: Childlike, needy or romantic. It steals feeling. I don't have to feel because they'll feel it for me.

MW: That is exactly the trouble. If it weren't so dangerous, I wouldn't get so fired up about it. Sentimentality robs us of our feeling. You see it on television. The news is rampant with sentimentality. Where is the real feeling? In relationships, people get trapped in sentimentality and run off into idealized affairs. It's just a way of avoiding their own reality and everybody else's. It's childish, not childlike.

CB: I associate sentimentality with addictive behavior, crying in your beer or acting overly expansive, like people do when they're on drugs.

MW: I agree. Neither sentimentality nor addictive behavior is grounded in the musculature of the body. Sentimental people feel sorry for people who really feel. Sentimentality looks down on life being fully lived. It's afraid of real feeling. Real feeling, on the other hand, blasts away sentimentality. Sentimentality cheapens the culture and betrays relationships. People who are terrified of suffering don't allow themselves to experience reality. They suffer neurotically, but they don't live the real conflict. And they're afraid to die so they're stuck. This is the problem in addictions. Mind you, I don't think life's all suffering.

CB: I don't hear that. You go to your island each year. You have a good time.

MW: I have a fabulous time. I think life is terrific. I wish I were thirty years old. Maybe there's another life. But, you see, there's a continual paradox. If you are in reality, yes, you suffer but you also experience the joy of reality, the sheer happiness of walking out and seeing that tree, that fantastic tree right there. Look at it, it's just a marvel! You know you're here, present in the moment! And with people, the same is true. You're giving energy; you're receiving energy. There's a continual flow.

So when you face death, when you know you've lived life, lived it to the fullest, you're ready to go on with a new chapter. If you haven't lived it, if you've never been here, never been present, I'm sure you'll be terrified of death because your whole life has been an absence. You've missed it. Well, by heaven, I don't intend to miss mine.

9

Marion Woodman in Perspective[*]

Analyst and author Marion Woodman is much in demand these days. When the former high school English teacher is not dividing her time between a busy practice in Toronto and her home in London, Ontario, she's racking up frequent-flyer points on speaking tours.

The acclaim still catches her unawares at times. Once, on her way to give a lecture in San Francisco, Woodman was coming in from the airport with her host when she noticed a long line of people huddled expectantly under umbrellas in a downpour. It made her wonder what she was missing.

"Who's in town?" she asked.

"Woodman," was the answer.

The wide appeal of Marion Woodman's work lies in part in its lively, imagistic prose that clothes intangibles in flesh and brings abstruse concepts down to earth, but what makes it stand out is that it addresses a profound need in all of us. Woodman is an analyst who specializes in bringing body and soul together in an age when more and more people are consigning their bodies to the junk-heap of addictions, and most don't even know they've got a soul.

It's an age she characterizes as one in which patriarchal values have become a parody of themselves. With the celebration of technology, the power dynamics of control and competition have escalated, cutting us off from feeling, from soul, and, ultimately, from the earth itself. To her, the crisis is self-evident in the spread of heart disease, in the rape of the planet and in our shabby treatment of our native peoples.

Noting that people's dreams are increasingly tormented by images of prison camps and vigilantes and armed strangers breaking into the home, Woodman points out that individual freedom, and the responsibilities that go with it, are in danger of degenerating into sheer fantasy.

And for her, any fantasy—whether of freedom or of a happy marriage— is an addiction. For her, an addiction is anything we do to avoid hearing the messages that body and soul are trying to send us—whether drugging ourselves into oblivion, drinking ourselves into a stupor, stuffing ourselves into obesity, starving ourselves into scarecrows or running smack

_____

[*] Newspaper article by Hans Werner, freelance writer, commissioned in 1990 by the *Toronto Star* (Toronto, Ontario). Unpublished.

into a heart attack in a mad chase after the next real estate flip.

Naturally, we prefer to pretend that none of this is really happening, or that there's some new drug or technological advance that will save us at the last moment. Woodman calls this living in a constant state of denial, which is what addicts do. We're constantly running away from ourselves for fear we might discover that, deep down where we really live, there's nobody home. And that would be altogether too painful. "The biggest problem in our society," she says, "is that people don't want to take responsibility for themselves."

Addicts can't endure pain, so they're usually pretty good at dumping it on someone else, like a relative or a partner. The ability of addicts to psychologically ambush their partners with victimizing, self-destructive games has given rise to the recently much-discussed problem of co-dependency and any number of self-help and confessional books aimed at liberating the co-dependent from the vicious circle that life with an addict traps them in.

While Woodman praises such efforts for at least getting people to think about the problem and giving the co-dependent some ground to stand on, she takes a rather deeper view. There are no quick fixes, she says, and relying on experts or books can become just another form of dependency. "Until we find the co-dependent in ourselves, we'll always make ourselves dependent on someone or something."

The same uncompromising insight lies behind her analysis of the ongoing struggle between the sexes, the subject of *The Ravaged Bridegroom*. According to Jungian theory, a man has a feminine side and a woman has a masculine one, and, just as a man's femininity is deformed by machismo, so is a woman's masculinity. It's this impaired masculinity that she projects onto her partner, and, likely as not, ends up with an alcoholic, an abuser; in short, a "ravaged bridegroom."

"We are all victims of the patriarchy," says Woodman.

A horrific instance of synchronicity brought this home to her in the midst of writing the book, when she turned on the TV one night and learned of the massacre of fourteen women at the Montreal Polytechnic. "Deep-rooted hatred of women, blasting out of a semi-automatic weapon," she wrote in a last-minute addition to the introduction of *The Ravaged Bridegroom*, "blasts open other arsenals of fear, bitterness and rage."

If men fear the feminine, so do women. Like a pair of facing mirrors, the two aspects of our psyche reflect each other's flaws; damaged masculinity partners maimed femininity. This is true in men as well as women.

For Woodman, matriarchy is no solution. Indeed, Jungian thought differs from some of the more radical feminist ideologies in holding that the patriarchy isn't *all* bad. As elaborated by Erich Neumann in *The Origin and Evolution of Consciousness,* the patriarchy was a necessary evolutionary step on the road to consciousness. For Woodman, the challenge facing us today is to discover what conscious femininity is, to find what she calls "the light in matter." In Jungian terms, the feminine is roughly equivalent to the soul.

Woodman says that children and teen-agers still have an inkling of what the soul is, yet the rising rate of teen-age suicide doesn't exactly surprise her. "If you aren't allowed to live your own life," she shrugs, "why bother?" Teen-agers feel, but their feelings are hedged round with the illusions of adults. Devils, after all, exist in our own psyches, and until we're brave enough to meet them there, we'll go on poisoning both the atmosphere around us and ourselves.

Woodman, who has known eating disorders from both sides—obesity and anorexia—knows what she's talking about. A United Church minister's daughter who throughout her youth moved around southwestern Ontario every five years, she eventually graduated with a degree in English, and subsequently taught literature and creative drama at London's South Secondary School for twenty-one years. Then her body collapsed and her teaching world came to an end.

Her search for answers, which included a journey to India to find a guru, led nowhere, until an inner drive, sparked by intensive work with a Jungian analyst in England, took her to the Jung Institute in Zürich. She spent five years there, returning to Canada in 1979 to set up her practice.

When I meet Marion Woodman at her office in the building that also houses Toronto's Jung Foundation, the first thing she says is, "Good morning," and the second, "I don't have a face."

She says people think she's anywhere between forty and seventy, "depending on when they see me." Then she sets up a compact mirror on her desk and proceeds to put on her make-up. I'm left to follow the dancing, rainbow-colored sunbeams streaming in through the stained glass window of the consulting room. Not that it looks much like an office. You're more likely to think you're in a venerable Rosedale mansion tastefully appointed with antiques—until a number of small but strategically-placed objects catch your eye.

There's a toy-sized pair of elephant tusks replete with toy-sized wheat sheaves and corn (which turns out to be an altar-piece from the Orient), a replica of a carving from a medieval cathedral, a Navajo medicine-man doll, a black madonna from Switzerland, a dancing walrus carved in bone, a reclining Buddha, and a bronze Paleolithic fertility god and goddess. On the wall behind her analyst's chair is a large reproduction of Leonardo's *St. Anne, the Virgin, and Child.* And there's a Miro she calls soul-writing.

"I have my soul objects in this room," says Woodman. "Analysands often don't know they've seen these images until they turn up in their own dreams. They're empowering archetypal images, dormant in the psyche."

If this sounds like our skulls are inhabited by a menagerie of phantom creatures, some religious and healing, some diabolical and destroying, it's not far from the truth. Archetypes are ways in which our essential energies (instincts) hold up a mirror to our consciousness. The diabolical ones are usually parts of ourselves we don't want to know about and are quick to unload onto somebody else. In other instances we may sell out the healing part—to a guru, an "expert," an evangelist, an analyst, a god . . .

"It's a natural process," says Woodman. "People project onto others those parts of themselves they don't know about."

Deep in this jungle dwells the soul—as best it can. Woodman notes that in patients' dreams the soul often turns up as a prisoner or an abandoned, undernourished child, like a Biafran orphan. But the psyche wants us to be whole, she insists, and itself speaks of an inner healing process. Each of us has his or her own unique psyche, and that already effectively limits the usefulness of self-help books and experts. The most an outside person (even an analyst) can hope to do is to help put the individual in touch with the inner process. "You have to follow your own images," says Woodman. "It's the only way to find out who you are."

Marion Woodman believes the soul likes to play as a child plays, that is, spontaneous, passionate, concentrated, delighting in just *being* through the senses. "If you can't enjoy what's in front of your eyes, life's not worth living." Descriptions of the anemia and listlessness that result from such a denial begin to sound a lot like the symptoms of what's been called the Yuppie Disease.

In a very real sense, says Woodman, body and soul are one. "We were given the body for a reason. If you keep trying to escape from your body, you'll kill it. That's true of our earth too. If you bury it under a garbage heap, it'll die." Throughout the ages, and in myths the world over, both earth and soul have always been considered feminine.

Woodman advises me to take a closer look at the dancing walrus. Cumbrously corpulent creature that he is, with one foot poised for a stompin' good time and flippers flailing in tune, he begins to take on a fluid gracefulness. Yup, he's pretty happy all right.

"It's a she," Woodman protests at my refusal to see what's in front of my eyes, "Look at her hips."

10

The Goddess Energy Is Trying To Save Us*

A. Robert Smith: I'm intrigued with the rising interest among psychotherapists in the spiritual dimension. Is this just new to me, this idea of the spiritual dimension being important for healing, or is it really something new to the profession?

Marion Woodman: I would say it's a natural growth process. The further you go in understanding yourself, the more you realize that the kingdom of God is within. And certainly if you are dedicated to the dream process, it will take you into the religious dimension. So that in finding the "I," you're also finding the "I" that is the God within. And in finding that, you are finding the God in other people, in plants, in animals—that animating soul that is in everything. You realize that while you are finding your own soul, you are finding also that you are *ensouled,* that there is one soul to which we all belong. When you work on the rotten foundations, which is what we do in therapy, you have to recognize your own rot. In order to get rid of rot, you've got to dig it up. At the same time, you're finding this magnificent soul that's buried beneath it.

Smith: Did psychologists always recognize the soul?

Woodman: Psyche means soul. Psychology is knowledge of the soul. It would be most ironic to explore the knowledge of what does not exist, though I realize some therapists do. Jung recognized soul. He talked about the soul in a man, the anima. And he recognized the spiritual dimension of dream images that connects a person to what he called the Self. The Self is the God-image within, like the golden ball in fairy tales. That golden ball takes you where you need to be led in order to find all the parts of yourself. Your goal is not perfection (which is a very one-sided attitude toward life) but your unique totality. During the process you may not know what you're doing, but as you look back you see that this unknown dream-maker has been taking you through a circuitous route to find your totality.

I do think a lot of people start out in therapy thinking they will find the blocks, that they will take the energy that's blocked in negative mother

---

* Reprinted from *Venture Inward,* vol. 6, no. 2 (March/April 1990), the magazine of the Association for Research and Enlightenment, which specializes in the work of Edgar Cayce. A. Robert Smith is the editor.

and negative father, for example, and release it from those complexes in order to make it available to the ego. But the journey becomes so fascinating that they tend to stay with it. The blossoming ego begins to relate to its own creativity, to the creation within. That process ultimately leads to surrendering to transpersonal energy, what Jung calls the Self.

Smith: There's a lot of talk among lay people who are into the New Age about raising their consciousness. You talk about a *new* consciousness. Is that something distinctly different in your mind?

Woodman: I believe there's a mutation going on. I'll tell you why. In the early stages of analysis, most of the time you're taking out the rot. You're confronted with your demons and those demons tend to seem more violent because as the ego becomes stronger it recognizes the full energy of the demonic.

I do believe evil exists. By evil I mean anything that would destroy your divine essence. In my experience with dreams there is an evil force that would smother the light of the soul if it could. But to answer your question, people who have fought their way to freedom from the complexes during five, six, seven years of analysis are often told in a dream that once they've got the courage to take the leap into the dark, their understanding of love is totally new. They *become* love, not that they *do* love but that they become love and live love.

I think of dreams of the Buddha, or a divine child, or a mature Christ—however the inner God is imaged—being in a group of students who are taught by an old man. They are learning to jump an abyss that they can scarcely imagine jumping. The fact that the God-image is in the group suggests to me that our understanding of the God within is moving into a whole new concept of what God is.

I think that the situation of our planet, our Mother Earth—the earthquakes, overpopulation, the destruction of the rain forests—are perils forcing us to a new consciousness of what matter is. It's not just black nothingness, opaque. There is energy within trying to be released. The French Impressionists captured that scintillating energy in their paintings of trees, grass, flowers. They *saw.* I think ordinary human beings are now waking up to see what is in their own matter, their own bodies, in terms of the larger consciousness in all matter. That awareness is coming in physics, mathematics, biology, theology, psychology. I call it the feminine side of God—God in matter. Matter as a metaphor of the Goddess.

Smith: You talked about the movement from power in our society or our world, the movement from the use of power to the use of love, and it struck me that that's been the issue for two thousand years.

Woodman: But we still don't know what it is.

Smith: Are we making any progress or are we still so wedded to power? Or do you see that—the connection between patriarchy and power—waning with the eruption of the goddess energy? Is this a time of change in that system of power?

Woodman: I would say the goddess energy is trying to save us. If we go on with our power tactics, we're going to destroy the earth. That's why we haven't got a long time to evolve. We're either going to make a leap in consciousness or we aren't going to be here. Sophia, Shakti, by whatever name we call her, is that wisdom deep down in all matter, pushing her way into consciousness, one way or another. We have to be aware of earthquakes and hurricanes. What are their rumblings trying to tell us?

I don't know if there's any change coming in patriarchy. It's war here, war there and power everywhere. And yet the Berlin Wall is down. It's down! What happened in China, in Tianamen Square, tragic as it was, was a push for freedom from patriarchy. All over the U.S.S.R. we see Gorbachev's incredible foresight. Last Nov. 11th, Remembrance Day in Canada, I was thinking about the First World War and how Canadians were marched in thousands over Vimy Ridge, slaughtered in hot blood as they came over the hill. It was insane to take battalions of men and put them up in front of guns to be shot. Surely we can never accept that kind of madness again. Fight to the death! By whose order? Yet people are willing to die for what they believe in. What is happening in Eastern Europe makes it very clear they will no longer tolerate patriarchal power.

Power is no longer going to work, except destructively.

That's also clear between men and women. We've been brought up on power; our parents and grandparents were brought up on power. We use power when we don't know we're using it, even people who want to do good. It can happen in psychotherapy—therapists who want to do good and have an image of what their clients should be. They think it's love that is motivating them as they tell their clients what to do. But that's power, not love. We do not know another person's destiny.

Love mirrors the other person, tries to see the *soul* of the other. Mind you, it's very hard to see because the soul long ago learned that if it shows itself it will get knocked down. When the child's soul tries to say something, the parents say, "That's not what you should say, that's not what you think." Or the teacher says, or the boss says, or the husband says, or the kids say, "That's not who you are." Gradually the soul goes underground. You see this in dreams where the dreamer is told to go and find what is buried in that black box in the back shed or some other hidden place. And sure enough this marvelous little creature is right there. I remember one dream where the woman puts her hand in that box and when she pulls her hand out she has a pet bird she loved as a child. It's just a little bird but it's still alive. She holds it on her hand and she's smitten with guilt because it's starving. But her tears falling on the bird transform it into a radiant little boy who says, "I only wanted to sing my song." That sort of dream can change your life—if you can remember you once had a song to sing.

Often in a session, the analysand is talking along as though he or she is very secure, and then I see the foot wiggling. And I say, "What do you think is wrong with your foot?" Or they will make an aside, and I'll say, "What was that?" They will deny it means anything. I say, "This is what I heard," and repeat it. They reply, "Yes, Marion, but . . ." Well, that's the soul manifesting in any way it can. It's learned just to slip through the cracks. It is so used to being struck down that it hides. Gradually it realizes it's safe to come out and it starts to push through. Then in dreams you see this exquisite creature. In the process of analysis, you see this shining little boy or little girl, and you know it is a divine child, the soul. There are other divine figures that appear in our dreams. They are creatures of light and they just cannot be denied.

A divine energy, the energy of creativity, is in the unconscious, and that energy is now pushing in a new direction. As long as people are pushing toward their own goals, driven by ego power, they are constantly fighting against the very energy that would give them their real strength.

Smith: You've said that a lot of men are shocked because they aren't really in touch with what's going on with women today. I have no doubt about that. But I'm wondering whether you can describe what you think is happening with women today in that sense?

Woodman: I think that more and more men are waking up. Most women, for centuries, have not expressed their real strength. They thought the feminine thing to do was to be subordinate, not to appear too strong because they might lose their man, not to appear too intelligent, to be the support for their men, and certainly to take on the victim role whenever necessary. That's true in men as well: their feminine is made victim of their masculine. Women do it to themselves, victimize their own femininity with their inner masculinity. Their inner betrayal is appallingly clear in dreams.

I think what's happening now is that women are learning more and more who they are. They are expressing their own values, their own experience of themselves. Even if it's going to cost them their relationship, they are putting their own sense of reality ahead of a relationship that is costing them their own identity. More than that, I think they are valuing their men more. They are seeing their men as human beings and loving them as human beings and saying, "I love you enough to say this is who I am and I will no longer pretend to be someone I am not. I will no longer try to live up to your image of me. I love you enough to be honest. This is who I am."

Men are still inclined to project their perfect inner woman onto their partner, so they can't understand what's going on when the outer woman does something their inner woman would not do. It comes as a mighty shock and often the man insists, "That's not who you are." A projection is a very real thing. It's real energy. If I'm projecting onto a man my adoration of him, that energy is like crutches holding him up. My energy is supporting him. If I take that projection away, suddenly he's without crutches, so it's a terrifying moment in a relationship; he not only loses the image he thinks he loves but loses the powerful support of the projection. Conscious women are pulling back the adoring projection. It hurts but it's much healthier. It lets a man be who he is, a human being trying to find himself, just as the woman is. It allows for real love.

Smith: It introduces reality into the relationship. That's really essential if there is to be equality in the relationship.

Woodman: So long as you're projecting your own inner image, you are entwined in your own narcissism. You are in love with yourself. If you persist in your unconscious projection, that's just neurotic self-indulgence. There is a terrible danger of falling into sentimentality. But real love actually opens the heart to loving someone totally other than you.

Smith: You've said, "Sentimentality robs us of our feeling." Explain what you mean by that.

Woodman: To me sentimentality is not genuine feeling. Sentimental people tend to ignore their own shadow, their own darkness. They cover up their real suffering with self-pity, for example, and stultify their own growth. Or they may focus their energy on another person who is trying to deal with genuine feeling, perhaps genuine evil, and because they're unable to face that in themselves they say, "Poor thing." They take a condescending attitude toward people who are fighting for their lives trying to get to their integrity. Sentimental people refuse to suffer. Real anger or real grief are put into cotton wool that smothers any possibility of transformation because they cannot stand the fire, and real feeling is tempered in fire. Real feeling moves into the conflict and holds the opposites until the new is born. Sentimentality fears the heat of passion. It takes a holier-than-thou attitude and pretends it knows no evil, feels sorry for anyone trapped in compulsive behavior. Nazis were sentimental. Children are not.

Smith: I have a feeling that a lot of people in our culture—American culture at least—are afraid of passion.

Woodman: Yes, I think our culture is terrified of passion because, at the core, people have been treated with power. They are like the little child whose father says, "What are you thinking about?" The child says, "Nothing." "Where've you been?" "Out." Look at the hostility there. The child is saying, "I don't trust you enough to tell you where I've been. And I'm certainly not going to tell you what I think." There's real alienation.

At the root of the fear of passion is fear of rage against those who ignored your boundaries and made you do what they wanted you to do. So rather than touch into that rage you just slide right over the top and pretend it doesn't exist. I see anger as a personal thing, rage as transpersonal. People are afraid of becoming angry because they are terrified of being possessed by rage. So they just skate. In their dreams they skate or ski, but it takes ice and snow to skate and ski, which means feeling is frozen. So rather than live in summer and spring, they just freeze. No gentleness, no flow! The heart is closed and they will tell you they feel nothing. They know what love is supposed to be, but as for feeling it, they never *felt* any emotion in their bodies. Is it any wonder heart attacks are our number one killer? Our own hearts are asking us to become conscious of what is happening in our matter. Earthquakes are asking us to become conscious of what is happening in our Great Mother's matter.

Smith: All this process seems to be in ferment in our society and leading us away from old patriarchal systems like the family. What's it leading to?

Woodman: I don't know. This is where I have to say, "I trust." And this is where I see the mutation. There is a leap here into the darkness. When you're in a relationship and you start into this process, you are not at all sure there will be anything left of your relationship in six months. If the partner can't move with you, you may look for someone who can. It changes the children, there's no question about that. As one person in the family comes to consciousness, the whole family is changed. Consciousness also changes the workplace. I know women who for years never told their boss what they thought. When they started to put forth their thoughts—they'd been thinking before but never said it—the boss said,

"You're not asked to think. You're here to do what I tell you to." It may cost them their job. So I don't know where it's going. It's chaos, that's for sure.

So many people who have lost their marriage or relationship go to their apartment at night and can scarcely put their key in the lock. They are flooded with loneliness. Darkness is all there is on the other side of that door. They project their own emptiness into the space. There is nobody home. It's a tragic waste of life. Here is where femininity is crucial. If you have worked hard on your complexes and you can tell the difference between your own voice and the destructive voices of your complexes, then you can pull in your own strength. You can say, "I am here. This place is not empty. I can fill it with my essence. This suffering is not meaningless. I trust that something new is being born from the chaos." Conscious femininity gives us the courage to trust in the moment without knowing what the goal is.

Smith: Is it the process itself you're trusting?

Woodman: Yes. I believe the psyche will try to heal itself if we give it a chance. It's that golden ball I talked about earlier, the god and goddess within that push us beyond our old boundaries. We have to cooperate, of course. We can't sit back and wait for it to happen because most of us are so crippled by old tapes, voices of parental complexes, that the minute our ego falters the old harangue starts, and within minutes the ego can collapse into unconsciousness. There is no sense talking about "being true to myself" until you are sure what voice you are being true to. It takes hard work to differentiate the voices in the unconscious. I spend at least an hour every day writing in my journal, separating out what is real from what is unreal, what stays, what goes. In the crises most of us are in, there is no time to waste in false clutter. We are challenged to break the old boundaries and leap beyond anything we ever imagined.

Smith: Is that the mutation again?

Woodman: Yes, the leap in consciousness. People get stuck in one frame of mind. They dream they are wearing their father's or mother's glasses, or child's play glasses. They are not seeing with their own eyes. The old frame has to be broken if we are going to *experience* what it is to be a citizen of a global village. We use that language but our responsibility to our little planet turning in space is still far from consciousness. If more of us put up the picture of Earth taken from the moon as an icon in our homes, maybe that would break the old glasses, the old hearing aids. Maybe we would have a glimpse of what we could be. Without a vision, we are stuck in obsolete patterns, like athletes who can't imagine themselves breaking a record. Because they can't imagine, they can't do it.

Our dreams give us the images for our personal lives and for the planet. Integrating those images takes hours of meditation and the humiliation of making fools of ourselves when we first try to put them into life. But, you know, once you've seen with new eyes and heard with new ears, you can't go back. However painful the path, you know you're in your own fire. You're learning what love is.

The divine lover, said Rumi, is cold in the fire, dry in the sea. He means that love brings matter to its consummation as consciousness. Fire as transformation, sea as creative matrix, not pain and drowning.

11

Journey to Conscious Femininity*

Sitting with author and Jungian analyst Marion Woodman in her uncluttered Toronto office in a two-story townhouse she shares with Freudian analysts and the Toronto Jung Foundation, I am struck by how ageless she looks. Though she is well into the second half of life, she appears soft and youthful. Her hair, sometimes pulled back and tightly braided, is now worn loose and carefree, like her two-piece, dark turquoise skirt and top accented by a strong piece of silver jewelry.

As she moves lightly about on the polished wooden floors of the office, which is tastefully decorated with a wall of bookcases filled with professional volumes and personal favorites whose bindings have been cracked many times, my eye is caught by a Leonardo da Vinci print, "Cartoon for St. Anne," which shows the child and the Virgin Mary sitting on the lap of her mother Anne. "It's always there behind me," says Woodman. "This drawing lives in me because it is an archetypal image of the conscious feminine embodied in the virgin. She accepts herself as part of the greater plan through which life eternally moves and she is firmly grounded on the lap of Mother Nature."

Whether she's working with a client one-on-one, addressing a conference brimming with people or speaking to the readers of her books, Woodman's insights into "spirit and matter and feminine consciousness" can mesmerize her listeners.

First and foremost she speaks about people becoming "fully embodied" in their lives, moving toward wholeness that Woodman calls "soul-making, or becoming ensouled." According to her, soul-making requires honesty, humility, a sense of humor, and the capacity to withdraw our projections, which are unconscious reflections of ourselves that we put on other people. Because Woodman herself embodies those qualities, her words have recently been reaching a larger and larger audience and having a tremendous impact, especially on women.

Last fall, on an unseasonably warm day in Washington, DC, I was one of more than two thousand people who crowded in to hear Woodman's keynote address at the ninth annual conference sponsored by Common

---

* Reprinted from *East West,* vol. 20, no. 11 (November 1990). Written by Caren Goldman, a freelance writer in Ohio.

Boundary, an organization of people in helping and healing professions that bridges spirituality and psychotherapy. Conference organizers had been obliged to turn away more than four hundred disappointed people who had come at the last minute in hope of attending workshops with Woodman as well as other leaders in the human consciousness field, such as Stephen Levine, Christina Grof and Barbara Brennan. Such a demand to hear Woodman speak or to be in one of her workshops is the norm, and her name is often among the list of presenters at conferences around the United States and Canada.

Norman O. Brown once said. "The aim of psychoanalysis—still unfulfilled, still only half-conscious—is to return our souls to our bodies, to return ourselves to ourselves, and thus to overcome the human state of self-alienation." In these terms, Woodman is giving women back their earth, their bodies, their true dignity as co-creators. She is showing women how to work beyond their impotence and rage and to discover for the first time in patriarchal history the immensity of their potential.

Woodman says, "The healing dimension of the unconscious is available to men and women who are willing to connect with powerful images from poetry, myth, personal dreams and personal experience. Images ignite the body electric that connects us to our inner reality."

Woodman's books have been described as "remarkable explorations of women's mysteries" that identify and bring new understanding to the causes of addictive behaviors.

While there are no easy cures for addictions, whether to food, alcohol, drugs or even perfection, Woodman believes that there is hope for all who are willing to take responsibility for their own lives and consciously strive to integrate body and soul. And, although Woodman concentrates on the psychology and attitudes of women in her books, what she has to say is, in fact, a celebration of the feminine in both men and women.

Werner Engel, New York psychiatrist and Jungian analyst, notes that the underlying hypothesis of *The Owl Was a Baker's Daughter: Obesity, Anorexia Nervosa and the Repressed Feminine,* Woodman's first book, published in 1980, "is that weight disturbances and eating disorders often have a meaning: that is, they are purposeful symptoms." He adds that Woodman's work is specifically directed toward practical procedures that can enable a woman to hear her bodily symptoms as symbolic representations worth exploring because they lead to an understanding of her instinctive femininity and the wounds it has suffered, inflicted not only by others, but also by herself.

The Owl Was a Baker's Daughter, a valuable introduction to Woodman's other work, expounds her theory that twentieth-century women have been living for centuries in a male-oriented culture which has kept them unconscious of their own feminine principle. "Now," she says, "in their attempt to find their own place in a masculine world, they have unknowingly accepted male values—goal-oriented lives, compulsive drivenness and concrete bread which fails to nourish their feminine mystery. Their unconscious femininity rebels and manifests in some somatic form."

Her second book, *Addiction to Perfection: The Still Unravished Bride,* published in 1982, is a study of the psychology and attitudes of modern women that offers a broader perspective on the themes in her earlier work. In it, Woodman continues to investigate women's mysteries through case material, dreams, literature and mythology, in food rituals, rape symbolism, Christianity, imagery in the body, sexuality and creativity.

In *Addiction to Perfection,* Woodman says she is "suggesting that many of us, both men and women, are addicted in one way or another, because our patriarchal culture emphasizes specialization and perfection. Driven to do our best at school, on the job, in our relationships—in every corner of our lives—we try to make ourselves into works of art. Working so hard to create our own perfection we forget we are human beings."

As a voice for women searching for their own inner voices, Woodman, more than any other contemporary writer, is responsible for such terms as "conscious femininity" as an influential concept. Woodman explains that this catch-all term means to speak with one's own inner voice through a process Jung referred to as "individuation," the conscious realization of one's unique psychological reality, including both strengths and limitations. She points to a passage in *The Pregnant Virgin,* published in 1985, which summarizes her idea that conscious femininity is, in fact, a means of articulating one's soul.

"The word 'feminine' has very little to do with gender, nor are women the sole custodians of femininity. Both men and women are searching for their pregnant virgin. She is the part of us who is outcast, the part who comes to consciousness through . . . mining our leaden darkness until we bring her silver out."

The Pregnant Virgin compares the process of psychological change to the metamorphosis of caterpillar to chrysalis to butterfly. It describes periods in the chrysalis when life as we have known it is over and we are, for all practical purposes, alone. No longer who we were, we know not who we may become. At such times, says Woodman, a thinking heart brings us closer to our inner virgin, "one-in-herself," forever open to new life, new possibilities—our own unique truth.

In *The Ravaged Bridegroom: Masculinity in Women,* Woodman delves into the psychological impact of patriarchy, and radically redefines masculinity in both men and women.

Woodman works with the unconscious both through dreams and the body. The language of dreams is the grammar of the unconscious, which repeats itself in body gestures. Together they make our deepest feelings known. Like a midwife, she works, as Jung would say, "not by imagining figures of light, but by making the darkness conscious."

"Often, when a woman first comes to me," Woodman says, "she will keep on a mask that covers up parts of herself so deeply buried she doesn't even know they're there. As her dreams take off her mask, we get to her essence. It's there that a woman can see the depth of pain, rage, shame and despair that has been covered up and led her to meaningless suffering, which in turn has driven her to escape through food, alcohol, drugs, sex."

Woodman, who has worked with individual clients for as long as eight years, notes that there are no quick fixes for making the darkness—one's shadow side—light.

"I think very few people grow into their own full stature. Those who are able to open to their own psychic and spiritual energy are often frightened by the thought of taking responsibility for it. If you take responsibility, and are strong enough to surrender to that energy, you surrender to a higher power. Many addicts or fatally ill people are forced into that path, and in the darkness they find a pinpoint of light. If they deny the agony of it, their spirit withdraws. To turn back is psychic death. Once you've acknowledged that energy, you can't turn back. It is a lifelong process that requires patience, trusting the timing of the psyche."

She recalls the depths of her own long, painful journey toward wholeness. She says that in the early stages of the process she personified D.H. Lawrence's question, "Are you willing to be sponged out, erased, canceled, made nothing . . . dipped in oblivion? If not, you will never really change."

During the early 1950s Woodman was an anorexic in her twenties who was, in her own words, "addicted to perfection." Although during that period she began a twenty-four-year career as a high school English teacher, she now says that even then she intuitively knew that the unconscious drive within her was toward death. Recognizing this, she waged a nine-year battle to bring her body back to health. But although the outer trappings of her addiction had been conquered, she was still carrying deep wounds.

When she was in her late thirties she entered a hospital with serious ᵗsical symptoms. "My body was being ravaged by a soul still seeking ᵗroper voice," she says. This time Woodman was determined to find that voice and hear what it had to say. In so doing, she began to discover that Jungian analysis would be a passage through the stormy seas of self-discovery.

She explains, "As women, we no longer have to be victims of our own biology. I was tyrannized for years by my biology. I was both tyrant and victim, and that is true of most women, because it's the only reality they know. At the age of twenty I was pretending and putting on a performance—wearing the mask I write about that so many women put on. I was striving for the perfection of a beautiful body and pure spirit. I set standards for myself that no human could reach. But what I didn't know then was that I was refusing to make the transition to womanhood. . . . It was actually a failed initiation rite, and the deepest levels of my psyche were saying, 'No' to cosmetic femininity. As the actress putting on a performance became more and more separated from reality, my addictive behavior filled the gap. Eventually the gap was so deep, the body, my body, couldn't hold it together."

The spiral that led Woodman through her addictive behavior into her calling as an analyst actually began at age five. As the daughter of a minister, Woodman says, "There's no question that my life in the parsonage was the root of my relationship to the unconscious. My whole world was baptism, wedding and funeral, and our home was forever pulsing with people's grief. I didn't find it morbid and I didn't know there were two worlds, theirs and the one I lived in. The archetypal world was real for me and I loved it."

She adds, "When I was a child I would spend hours hiding in the church, waiting for God to come. I would hear these creaks, and I was terrified God was really coming. There was an open vulnerability on my part, and my inner 'young masculine,' which is another way of saying my creative psyche, was telling me life and ideas were fascinating.

"When I got to school, however, most people found my creative energy impossible to deal with. I found myself living in a cage. My teachers appreciated my performance when I acted the way they wanted me to, but they didn't hear me . . .

"The other side of my frustration and anger was the opposite—immense joy. I truly loved literature and had started to keep a journal when I was eight. Through those early years I was holding my fingers on the pulse of reality. During my teenage years, however, I didn't have the physical energy to both pretend and continue to live my own reality. By the time I was twenty I was anorexic."

Woodman believes that when an addicted individual, such as one with an eating disorder, begins to live with a minimum of food or fasts, the person's spirit is held by a tenuous thread. Quoting such authors and poets as Sylvia Plath, Emily Dickinson and Virginia Woolf, whose works explore the boundaries of spiritual longing and physical demise, Woodman uses her own experiences to help persuade women troubled with all types of addictive behavior to realize that one does not have to leave this earth to have a subtle body that has that "light"—an all-knowing wisdom—in its cells.

"It is utter foolishness to try to escape from your body in order to be in touch with the riches of the unconscious," she says. "Addicted people yearn for freedom. They want to get out of their bodies and be someplace else. For me, it's important to experience my subtle body here on earth. Gradually, we can bring consciousness to the wisdom in our bodies. That's what I mean by releasing energy from matter, thus allowing the conscious body (the energy body) to become a chalice for the reception of spirit. That's true feminine consciousness."

In 1968, while still a school teacher, Woodman went on a worldwide search for a guru. She never did reach her predetermined goal in India, but she was open along the way to other possibilities, one of which turned out to be a year of Jungian analysis in England. There she unexpectedly discovered her true path after meeting the Jungian analyst E.A. Bennet, who helped transform her intellectual journey into a journey of the soul.

Bennet was in his eighties when they met.

"I had been seeing him for about six months, and I was still trying to be a good girl. On Christmas Eve I learned that my dog, who was in Canada, had been killed. I decided not to waste my six o'clock session that evening talking about my dog and I arrived as well organized as usual.

"At the end of the hour, Dr. Bennet sat and thought and asked me what was wrong. 'Nothing,' I said, as I was putting on my coat. When he said I hadn't been there during the session, I told him my dog had died.

"He began to weep! I was astonished! He was weeping over my dog! He asked me how I could waste Christmas Eve chattering when my soul animal had just died. All of a sudden I found that his feeling was making me feel what I was doing to my feminine soul. We cried together. That's when my analysis truly began."

By 1979 Woodman had finished her training at the C.G. Jung Institute in Zürich, and she returned to Canada as a certified analyst.

In her contribution to a recently published collection of essays,[*] Woodman discusses the role of the conscious crone in feminine growth. The

---

[*] *To Be A Woman: The Birth of the Conscious Feminine* (Los Angeles: Jeremy P. Tarcher, Inc., 1990).

crone is someone who has gone through crossroads after crossroads; she has been there.

"Symbolically, crossroads represent moments in our lives where the unconscious crosses consciousness, where the eternal crosses the transitory; in other words, times and places where a higher will demands the surrender of our egos. The crone has gone through many crossroads; she has reached a place of conscious surrender where her ego demands are no longer relevant. She is a surrendered instrument, and therefore detached."

Woodman explains:

"I don't know any other way to live now. My dreams provide the rudder for my life. My work is to find my own authenticity and then to surrender that to a higher purpose, which I call Sophia/Christ. It is at the place of wounding that we find ourselves connected to each other in love, and it is here that I open to loving other people, loving the planet, loving the cosmos. I think the future of our planet depends on human beings discovering their own light, becoming conscious of the universe as one soul."

12

A Meeting with Marion Woodman*

Pythia Peay: At the age of forty-five you made a sudden career shift, leaving your position as a high school English teacher to become a Jungian analyst. Can you tell me something about that period in your life?

Marion Woodman: I had gone to India in 1968, thinking I would find a teacher there. I did not find the teacher I expected, but the experience in India changed my life. Then I went to England two years later with my husband, who was on sabbatical. By sheer synchronicity a friend gave me the telephone number of a Jungian analyst by the name of E.A. Bennet. I stepped into his office and knew I had found the teacher I had been looking for. I stayed with him for a year, ran out of money, then went home and taught school for three more years. It was the best teaching of my life; but I had made an inner commitment to go to Zürich for further analysis as Dr. Bennet was no longer practicing. So at the end of that three year period I resigned my job—in January, because I knew it would be impossible to resign at the end of the year. The experience of leaving was very traumatic.

Peay: Why was that so traumatic?

Woodman: I'd taught school there for twenty-one years, *loved* teaching school, and had an ongoing creative theater project. The students loved it, and they were very upset about losing it. I had a close bonding with the students. I was also married; I didn't want to give up my home in London, Canada, and my mother was still alive at the time. I didn't want to give up all that was important to me. But on the last day of May, which was the last day for turning in my resignation, the principal came and asked me if he should tear up my resignation. As it turned out, he hadn't handed in my resignation to the board because he said he knew I wasn't going to leave after twenty-one years. So I thanked God in my heart, and said thank heaven, I don't have to go, thank you, thank you for letting me out of that little bargain.

That night I was in the emergency room of the hospital. My body had started to do very strange things. The doctors couldn't find the cause, and I

* Reprinted from *The San Francisco Jung Institute Library Journal,* vol. 11, no. 1 (1992). Pythia Peay is a freelance journalist in Bethesda, Maryland.

had no idea—except I knew I was going to Zürich. My husband told the principal that my resignation stood. I had come to the end of teaching. I didn't want to believe it. I think that so long as I had a big adolescent in me, I understood the kids' language, I understood their music, I understood the way they thought. But it was increasingly obvious to me that I was losing that close understanding. God had another idea for what I was to do and it was essentially that breakdown in my body that forced the issue.

Peay: It seemed your husband was also insightful enough to recognize what was really going on for you.

Woodman: He recognized that it had to be, that it was not a personal choice. But I did not go to Zürich to become an analyst, I went for further analysis. At that point I was simply trusting in the guidance of my dreams. I tried my best to think there might be another way—but there was no other way. So I lived out my destiny.

Peay: How did your dreams point you in the direction of your destiny?

Woodman: My dreams told me three years before that that was the direction I was to go in. Then I had other dreams that January that repeated the same theme: you know the direction you're meant to take. So I followed those dreams—but then I thought maybe I was going to be released from my bargain!

Peay: So you gave up teaching, and without even knowing what you were going to "be" professionally, you went to Zürich for analysis.

Woodman: Yes, but I still hoped I'd go back to teaching. Teaching was my calling and so I always thought, up until my second year in Zürich, that I would go back to teaching. But as I watched all my friends at the Institute prepare for their examinations, it seemed to me that they were getting a tougher tempering than I was. So I decided to take the exams. That went well, so I took the final exams two years later and that led to being an analyst.

Peay: Are there similarities between being a teacher and an analyst?

Woodman: I try to give my analysands the tools they need to interpret their dreams, and to walk with them on their road. Where the teaching really comes in is in the workshops. My experience as a school teacher is very valuable when I'm standing up in front of a group of people trying to explain ideas and opening up new avenues of thought.

Peay: Do you believe now, after what you went through yourself, that radical, personal transformation is possible for others?

Woodman: I do. I think if it's your destiny, you will find the resources inside you to do it. It is extremely painful, and you have to trust with everything in you, because you don't know where you're going, and you don't know what the cost is going to be. And the cost is high. But I would say that my whole concept of life changed in India. That was the beginning of my radical transformation.

Peay: How did your encounter with India, as an entirely foreign culture, change you?

Woodman: In India I had no control over anything. I was alone. People would say good evening in the morning and call me sir. Details like that, combined with the maelstrom of life in the streets, left me with this sense that everything was chaos. I either had to give up or die, because I was getting into one situation after another where I was constellating death. By trying to control I was making the situation worse—I was actually becoming more and more powerless. I couldn't make any decisions, and if I did it was the wrong decision. Finally, I had to go with the flow of things and, for me, that felt like total giving up. Because I had been a very efficient and well-organized teacher. Everything had to go click-click-click. But in India that was broken in me, crushed in every possible way. Then I began to realize that there was another force, like riding on top of a wave.

I really didn't have to do anything except stay on top of the wave, and the wave would take me where I needed to go. It was a most remarkable feeling! Instead of constellating death I began constellating love on all sides. I came to love the Indian people. I thought that I could have been one of those little children sleeping on the street. I began to realize what an incredible gift it had been to have been born in Canada, and the responsibility involved in that, and I began to take that responsibility to heart.

Peay: What was that responsibility?

Woodman: To live up to my true potential. I had been giving to my students, but it was still a very narrow world. I was very moved when I saw the suffering in India, and the love that that suffering could unleash. I was recognized in India, in an extraordinary way, because I am an intuitive by nature. Indians recognized that and responded to that side of me. I felt seen, in a way that my own culture rejected. I was able to trust my own intuition and it opened my heart to something totally new flowing through— and I wanted to go with that flow. It was a gift. But as you know, I had to be brought to the bottom. It was chaos inside and chaos outside.

Peay: In *The Pregnant Virgin,* you say that you were actually rescued on the street by a woman, a stranger, who recognized you were in a severe state of culture shock.

Woodman: She picked up a bag of bones. I've often thought of that American woman. She asked me if I was alone, I said yes, and fainted dead away. She picked up that bag of bones from the street and put it in a taxi and took it with her—she had no idea what she had. She took me to her hotel, determined I was going to go home. But I knew I had to stay.

Peay: How long did you stay?

Woodman: Three months. The real change came in my own hotel room during a severe sickness with high fever. I had lost consciousness. When I came to, my body was on the floor and my soul was on the ceiling. I had to make the choice there, whether to come back into my body or whether to go. And there really was a choice. When I had been anorexic, I always thought that when the choice finally came—I would leave. But when it happened, and I was already on my way out, I wanted back in. The thing that saved me was my dog.

Peay: How did your dog save you?

Woodman: I perceived my body as a dog. I am very fond of dogs and I loved my dog. And I saw this patient, loyal thing lying on the ground. Breathing.

Peay: Your body?

Woodman: Yes, but to me it was a thing. I could see it going up and down. And I thought, "Stupid thing, it doesn't even know it's dead, and there it is waiting for me to come back, just like my little Duff would wait." And I thought, "I wouldn't betray him, but I would betray my own body." Suddenly I realized what that betrayal meant—to have been given a life and then decide it's not worth living. That seemed to be an ultimate betrayal. I thought, "I wouldn't do this to my own dog, and I can't do it to my own body." I was overcome by the sweetness of this patient thing trusting that I would come back. I decided then to take responsibility for the life I was given—it wasn't mine to throw away.

Peay: How long did you struggle with anorexia?

Woodman: Well, I would say, in its worst form, about six years. It was all part of being efficient and organized and wanting to belong to the collective in a "thin" way. It was also part of wanting light. I wanted light. It was the longing for God. And when you're starving or dancing all night, as I did in those days, it's amazing how much light you can bring into the cells of your body.

Petty: You used to dance all night?

Woodman: I taught in northern Ontario for awhile. Where I lived the real dancers didn't get going until about one in the morning.

Petty: You went to discos?

Woodman: No, no. Ballroom and square dancing—grand square dancing. During the winter there was nothing else to do but dance at night. Three nights of the week I danced from nine at night till 5 a.m.—and loved it. Weight fell off me. But I was addicted to that sense of euphoria. I still love dancing.

Petty: But since you're not anorexic anymore, and you don't dance the nights away, you must find that euphoria in a different way.

Woodman: Yes. But I don't think it's euphoria I'm looking for now. Euphoria is false. The high that comes from being anorexic, the weightless feeling that came from dancing and not eating, was a false euphoria. It was a death trip. Happy as I was on my way to suicide, it wasn't real at all. It was a straight betrayal of life. Now my journey is to the reality of the light—God as embodied consciousness. My whole desire then was to escape, now it's to go deeper and deeper into life.

Peay: We hear so many psychospiritual phrases these days. What does "embodied consciousness" mean? Are you talking about a state of consciousness that is different from the transcendent state experienced in meditation?

Woodman: I think God is that too. "Embodied consciousness" is my own phrase, reached through fifteen years of hard work. I had to come to God the other way around. I had to go through the body to find the Goddess. To me the feminine side of God is consciousness in matter. The wisdom in the body; the light in the cells; the subtle body. For me, that subtle body within my physical body is the receiver that can receive that transcendent experience of the divine. Before my experience in India I had no subtle body to receive the spirit; I was not conscious below the neck.

Peay: All your books deal in one way or another with eating disorders. Was it your own personal experience with anorexia that led you to write on that subject?

Woodman: Of course.

Peay: You were one of the first Jungians to write about eating disorders. Is that correct?

Woodman: Yes, I was one of the first. I did it because I had to. In Zürich I wrote my thesis on Emily Dickinson, who was also obsessed with light. When I finished I had a dream saying, "Now you can start your thesis." Because I still had not dealt with my own shadow. I took that dream very seriously, and wrote another thesis on binging and anorexia. That turned out to be *The Owl Was a Baker's Daughter.*

Peay: There was quite a response to that book.

Woodman: Yes there was. And that was just the tip of the iceberg compared to what I know about it now.

Peay: Your books are written within an obvious Jungian context. How has the Jungian psychological point of view added to our understanding of eating disorders?

Woodman: My Jungian analysis allowed me to understand the complexes that give rise to eating disorders metaphorically. The body sends messages from the unconscious just as dreams send messages. I think eating disorders are related to a problem with the mother. Mother is related to nourishment, cherishing, sweetness—food is a metaphor for mother. So that in any family where there's a person with an eating disorder, if the family cares, they are all going to have to come face to face with their relationship to the feminine. I am convinced that the feminine is making her way into our culture through the back door; one of those back door routes is through eating disorders. When you're really following the analysand's dreams in an eating disorder, you begin to see that an eating disorder is a religious problem.

Peay: What do you mean by a "religious problem?"

Woodman: It's a longing for the archetypal mother. The sweetness, the cherishing, the acceptance, the mirroring by the missing mother—I mean mother with a big M. It isn't just a longing for the personal mother, but a longing for the Mother Goddess, a being in whom you can have total trust.

Peay: So when you say that eating disorders are linked to a repression of the feminine in our culture, you mean the feminine side of God, or what you call the Goddess?

Woodman: Yes. I call her Sophia. What is paramount in our culture is patriarchal power. When I described to you how efficient I was, how organized with calendars and clocks, I was describing a power-driving masculinity that left no room for feminine meandering. I had to be in control. That ends up being power, will power without a strong ego underneath. But I would not have seen it at the time. I wanted A's at university, I wanted to be top in everything that had to do with the mind. The feminine isn't interested in being at the top: she's dedicated to life in the moment, she takes time to look at trees and flowers; she takes time to build depth relationships, takes time to be carried by that other force that trusts that there's inherent meaning to this life. I had lost touch with that trusting side of myself. As a child I had known it, but the longer I was in school the further I was away from it.

Peay: If it is a religious problem that lies at the basis of an eating disorder, then what are the religious distinctions between the struggles of an anorexic, a bulimic, and someone who is obese?

Woodman: It seems to me that obesity and anorexia are two sides of one coin. The binger and the anorexic are the extremes. The anorexic is going for Light—she dreams everything white. The thing that's after her in her dreams is white, sterile, Luciferian light. Whereas the binger is trapped in darkness. Concretized matter is pulling her down. Her body is dark, opaque, unconscious matter. The dream demon that is chasing her is black. They are two different kinds of dream images, both trying to escape from life, but at different poles. The binger needs to be grounded and food will ground her. When you have emotions that are out of control—fear and rage for example—you eat chocolate, you swallow those emotions that are threatening to sweep you right out of yourself. You can push them down, and as you get fatter and heavier you are grounded, but grounded in unconsciousness, if you're using food to escape.

Peay: That image of someone swallowing their emotions seems to fit with the cultural notion of the fat person as complacent and sweet.

Woodman: Yes. Often they have decided to perform for the culture. Whatever the culture wants, they will be sweet and complacent and all the time hate themselves for not being who they are. They are often raging inside. The anger has concretized on the body. The fat body is the rebel against the thin, collective ideal. The anorexic, however, is into spirit. The hardest thing in dealing with anorexics is that once they start to eat they don't experience that spiritual intensity so vibrantly.

Peay: And they have to give that up?

Woodman: They have to give that up. "If this is what life is," they say, "it's boring." Whereas the binger has come to the point of intensity and has chosen to eat to dampen it, bulimics swallow it and then can't stomach what they've swallowed. Metaphorically they have swallowed the mother they yearn for—they get her into the stomach and out she comes in vomit.

Peay: These distorted relationships with food seem to be pointing to deep cultural problems with the feminine.

Woodman: I think the spiritual feminine is practically nonexistent in our culture. People simply do not like the feminine. They are terrified to let go. Into what? Nothingness? So she has to come in the back door, through eating disorders or other addictions. Eating disorders reveal an enormous paradox. On the one hand, the spiritual feminine is so desired, and on the other, we are burying ourselves in our own concretized matter. You can't just pretend that two hundred pounds isn't sitting in front of you.

Generally speaking, the feminine is thought of as irrational and stupid. Women will come out with a feminine statement and then say, "Oh, that was stupid to say that." It's the circuitous way the feminine moves. She moves like a snake, back and forth and around and deep and around. I am often criticized for the way I speak, because it's not orderly, it's not going toward a goal, it's not linear. I purposely do not lecture that way anymore because for me it's very boring to know exactly where I'm going. I love the pleasure of the journey. I have a plan in my head; there are three or four points I want to make—but exactly how those are going to be expressed, I don't know. I trust that something will happen. Most people are terrified of spontaneity. They don't know how to be in the now so they'll do anything to follow a preconceived plan. This is the exact opposite of the feminine, which lives in the present.

Peay: How do you treat those who come to you for help with their eating disorders?

Woodman: I don't look specifically at the problem because I see it as a symptom of something much deeper. So I work with the dreams. Metaphorically speaking the person is usually living in a concentration camp, brutalized by Nazi officers—the power drive within and without. The feminine can barely exist with that kind of brutality. I have workshops where I try to help people relate to their body in a loving way, not in a keep-fit way. I'm not saying that keeping fit isn't loving, but it is important to know the body and respect it, to honor it as a sacred temple. I try to bring body and psyche together.

Peay: How does the body work you do with your clients differ from the fitness approach to body work?

Woodman: I work with the psyche through dreams, and with the body through dreams and workshops, and with the voice through breath.

Peay: How does this differ from keeping fit?

Woodman: It's working with imagery, it's working with soul. The images are pictures of the soul and we use those as the bridge between psyche and body. Some people don't like to be in workshops, they prefer individual body work. So they do Feldenkrais or yoga, whatever they choose. But almost everybody in my practice is doing both body work and dream work.

Peay: In one of your books you describe body work and dream work as very similar. The body gives us metaphorical images and messages from the unconscious in the same way dreams do, we just haven't been taught to interpret those messages.

Woodman: We can interpret them if we take time to listen to our body, to the images that come up. If we concentrate on our heart, often a gorgeous flower will manifest. But images also come that aren't quite so beautiful as flowers—they can be quite diabolical. They make us face the other side of ourselves. The point is we are flesh and blood and often we don't experience the reality of a psychic image until we feel it in our body.

Peay: You ask the question in *The Owl Was a Baker's Daughter,* "Is the repressed god that was somatized as hysteria in the early part of this century now appearing in anorexia and obesity?" I understood that hysteria used to be linked to sexual repression. Is there a connection between eating disorders and sexual repression?

Woodman: Well, once an eating disorder begins to heal, a sexual problem may emerge. A woman who is relating to her body becomes attractive to men, and as soon as men begin to pay attention to her—or to touch her—suddenly she starts to eat again and puts on weight. Often a woman with a profound eating disorder is about one year old. The soul went underground at about the age of one; the little girl started to perform and be what people wanted her to be. So when the weight comes off you have a one year old trying to relate to a man, and she simply can't do it. So you've got to allow that one year old to catch up, in a spiritual sense, to what she is in her physical body. Then she will be able to relate to men. Often the body functions as a suit of armor against sexuality.

Peay: How does that work with an anorexic?

Woodman: There you've got bone instead of fat acting as armor—in a real anorexic. Some people are anorexic because it's stylish. But real anorexics genuinely forget to eat, or simply can't.

Peay: Most men and women are very confused about their sexuality.

Woodman: It seems to me that to receive a penis there has to be a really profound sense of who you are, in order to allow yourself to be penetrated by another human being. A woman has to have a real sense of her own presence to surrender into full orgasm because she is entering into an altered state of consciousness. I think the fear of surrender in the anorexic epitomizes the fear of the feminine—and that's the feminine in men as well. The feminine in men is more terrified than the feminine in women.

Peay: How does that fear affect a man when it comes to sexual relationships?

Woodman: In human sexuality I think of the yin-yang symbol. The yin has some yang in it and the yang's got some yin. In the sexual act you have a continual moving of that circle so that the woman experiences her full masculine and feminine and the man experiences his full masculine and feminine. That's real love-making, where you experience the wholeness within yourself through the person you love. But if the woman moves into her yang and the man becomes frightened of her assertiveness, which he may experience as aggression, he won't be able to accept it. He will withdraw and become impotent.

Peay: I sometimes feel more sadness from men these days than women.

Woodman: I do too. As men begin to realize what they've done to their feeling side they are heartbroken. Literally—heart disease is the number one killer in this society. Because for so long the heart has carried the burden unconsciously it finally breaks. Now that's starting to come to consciousness. Men and their partners are going to suffer because consciousness brings suffering.

Peay: No one seems to have the slightest idea what the rules are in relationships anymore.

Woodman: There are no rules. And that's good, because we've been thrown into a completely new ethos. The old one is useless, hopeless.

Peay: What do you mean by the old ethos?

Woodman: Patriarchy. A patriarchal society is based on power, control over others. Lots of women are just as bad patriarchs as men. Worse. I think the whole planet is moving from power to love. But the agony involved to make that move! Because we have been brought up on power, that is the ethos we understand. If our parents or our teachers or our boss controlled us, then that's what we understand as life. So the old relationships have to become chaotic in order to find anything new. And they are chaotic. But I think it's pretty exciting. You say what you think in a situation and the other person's quite shocked. Then the next time you meet there's something totally new going on between you. Each one puts forward just a little bit more and often the person you thought was standing there isn't there at all—there's somebody totally different from the one you imagined. It's like therapy.

Peay: That does seem to be what is emerging—the therapeutic process as a basic part of relationship. The so-called conscious relationship or the marriage-as-therapy model.

Woodman: That's right. In the therapeutic situation the person who sat in front of me last week is different from the one sitting there today. However, there's a difference when you could lose a relationship because you're growing so fast. No matter how much you change, you know you're not going to be put out of analysis.

Peay: How can that therapeutic process be handled in a relationship without two people becoming burdened with each other's problems?

Woodman: Or ripping each other to pieces. I think that rage and other dark holes have to be handled in the therapeutic situation, not in the relationship. You work on your rage with your therapist before you talk to your partner about it.

Peay: In other words, you bring into the relationship the fruit of what you've learned about yourself in therapy.

Woodman: Essentially, yes. I'm not suggesting that couples shouldn't be straight and honest with each other, and acknowledge their fear, anger or whatever. But the sheer rage that tears another person's guts out has no place in a relationship. Because it's not personal, it's transpersonal. The ego is no longer present when anger becomes rage.

Peay: Haven't we gone too far with trying to work out this issue in terms of addiction?

Woodman: But we are an addictive culture.

Peay. But suddenly everything has become an addiction, to the point where we've become addicted to addictions. People say, "I can't drink, I'll become addicted to alcohol; I can't eat, I'll become addicted to food; or I can't love you, I'll become addicted to you."

Woodman: That's just crap, a real cop-out. People who talk like that don't want to take responsibility for themselves. The thing is, if you're an addict with food, you're going to be an addict with money and an addict with relationships. Addicts have a way of existing.

Peay: What is that way? What is an addictive personality?

Woodman: I think addictive personalities are unconsciously committed to self-destruction. They are dependent. They have enormous energy, which they put blinders on, and just go for something. They deny their inner emptiness so they run as fast as they can to try to escape. That's addictive behavior to me. It's the same thing with relationships. With a dependent relationship you just keep running as fast as you can and pretend you're not dying at the center of it.

Peay: How can one differentiate between what is the longing for a secure, stable relationship and a dependent relationship? Isn't a certain amount of dependency part of a normal human need?

Woodman: I would say that so long as you don't have a sense of your own totality, you are going to look for your wholeness in another person. It's the same principle with food—you'll look for your totality in food, or alcohol or drugs. If you are looking for somebody else to complete you, you are bound to become an addict in terms of relationships. The task, as I see it, is to try to become a whole person so that you are capable of loving another human being.

Peay: But how many of us are whole, complete individuals? It seems like an unrealistic expectation to bring to a relationship.

Woodman: Well, none of us is entirely whole. But if we at least envision ourselves as whole then we don't abandon ourselves to other people and expect them to make us happy.

Peay: So it's the process of becoming whole and autonomous that's really important.

Woodman: Yes, it's the process. The less you take responsibility for yourself the more dependent you are on another human being. When you're young, you project your inner mate onto another person. That's automatic, unconscious. You can't help it, it happens. You fall helplessly in love the first time because you're in love with your own projection. Gradually, you recognize there is a being inside you that is your own other half, someone quite different from the man or woman you love out there. But that realization doesn't come until much later; you have to go through a whole series of projections, each time recognizing more of yourself.

Peay: What is a projection?

Woodman: It's like an arrow. It's a bundle of psychic energy that sees something out there that it's attracted to and the arrow is automatically fired—bang!—and if the other person has an arrow coming at you, that is called falling in love. And it's a straight neurosis. But it is part of psychic growth. As time goes on, you begin to realize that all these men, or women, you are so fatally attracted to are all very much alike at their core. You're really falling in love with your own projection each time. Gradually it gets through to you that it's not the other person you're in love with, but part of your own self that you're projecting onto that person. It's those projected parts of ourselves that we have to pull back. A lot of women project their mother onto a man. It's all a bag of confusion!

Peay: What do you mean by having to "pull back" projections?

Woodman: That is the most painful, agonizing process in the world. Because you have to recognize that what you thought was out there in another person is not out there, but inside yourself. Most people experience pulling back a projection as isolation, as being cut off from the outer world. But if you have loved a man and you have projected your inner god onto him, you have to recognize that he isn't a god after all. The real god is inside. You have to recognize the illusions, the delusions and the pain of human limitation. Then gradually it dawns on you what a huge mistake you've made.

Peay: What happens then?

Woodman: When you're able to recognize that it's your god you've been projecting, or, in a man's case, the goddess, you learn to hold that divinity within. Then you're able to ask yourself, "Do I love that human being?" And you may find out that you do. That this man *is* sharing the journey with you, and he's put up with (dare I say) all your shit (that's how dreams image it), and you've put up with his, and there the two of you are, walking through life, together. There's something noble in his suffering. There's something noble in your own suffering. You're not leaning on each other. You're walking parallel paths, you're not holding each other up. That's a marvelous thing, to love another human being like that.

Peay: But to do that, if I hear you right, you have to be able to distinguish the human in your partner from the divine in yourself. You have written about the importance of differentiating between the sacred and the profane. The institutions, the rituals, that were once there to help us mark those boundaries are no longer there.

Woodman: Yes. There's a terrible danger of trying to make everything sacred. Sacredness has to do with the archetypal world. When you move into sacred space you purposely let the ego go in order to drop into the archetypal realm. For a moment, in the mass, for example, you purposely let yourself go into the incredible experience of identifying with the god or goddess. You are a much bigger person when you come back with that knowledge; your ego is expanded. But if you imagine you are a god, and nothing in your brain clicks to say, "I am not a god, now I'll go back to my human limitations," you can become crazy. That is one of the biggest dangers in our culture. Because kids watch television and identify with what they see, they can't tell the difference between the personal and the transpersonal.

Peay: Is that because they haven't been given the tools to discover their own unique identity?

Woodman: Partly. So they identify with whatever is on the screen, and you get cases like a man identifying with John Lennon and when John Lennon doesn't fulfill the projected image, he's shot. That's archetypal identification. But if you can separate the archetypal dimension from the human then you can say, "Last night I was in transcendent space. I was a goddess and I felt myself loved by a god. But this morning I wash the dishes and eat my oatmeal."

Peay: Very hard to do . . . (*no*)

Woodman: Yes, but you have to be able to separate the human from the divine. Otherwise you are constantly involved with inflation, and inflation leads to addiction—trying to escape the dishes and the oatmeal.

Peay: You often describe the behavior of people with eating disorders as ritualistic—the special clothes they wear, the "icy altar" of the refrigerator, the Dionysian frenzy accompanying binges, and so on. How does this mythical frame of reference help us to understand addictive behavioral patterns?

Woodman: I always try to grasp the metaphor at the root of an addiction. That varies. With food, it can be mother; with alcohol, spirit; with cocaine, light; with sex, union. Mother, spirit, light, union—these can be archetypal images of the soul's search for what it needs. If we fail to understand the soul's yearning, then we concretize and become compulsively driven toward an object that cannot satisfy the soul's longing.

Peay: So once you've identified the metaphor behind the addiction, then you can find other ways of satisfying the need for metaphor? If there's a need for light, you could replace cocaine with . . .

Woodman: Music, for example. And union . . . you could go to the inner god who may want you to paint, dance, sing or write with him. There is immense joy in creating.

Peay: Mythology plays a very important part in the Jungian therapeutic process. What is your definition of a myth?

Woodman: I would say it is the soul's journey, told in a universal story. Let's take a feminine figure, Medusa. In the Greek myth, she turned those who looked at her to stone. Many women look in the mirror today and see Medusa—in two hundred pounds of fat, or the ten pounds of fat they can't get rid of.

Peay: So Medusa is the angry feminine?

Woodman: Angry and insatiable. The snakes on Medusa's head keep writhing, not knowing what they want—but they want more and more and more. Women obsessed with Medusa look in the mirror and are turned to stone by what they see. It is tragic because they are faced with their own rejection of themselves, so they can never be satisfied. They turn everything around them to stone too. There's a living myth, right there.

Peay: What is this mysterious power behind a myth?

Woodman: Myth gives meaning to what would otherwise be a two-dimensional life. It brings in the divine element.

Peay: A lot of people seem more comfortable with imagery from the ancient Greek myths than they do with images from the Judeo-Christian tradition. Why is that?

Woodman: It's too close. It's easier to talk about what is far distant. We have to remember that most of the ancient myths prefigured what developed later. But for most people it's very hard to talk about Christ as myth, or Mary Magdalene as myth. Some people can't even deal with the word

God. They'll talk about the Greek gods or the Egyptian gods but *God*—not that word.

Peay: In *Addiction to Perfection* you write that if all the traditional religious structures were intact your waiting room would be empty. You go on to say that each person must weave together his or her own inner home out of the wreckage of the traditional structures with the images that have the most personal meaning. Is this construction of a spiritual center a way in which we can connect to myth in today's world?

Woodman: What a person needs is a bigger framework than the smaller personal framework, because a personal framework can become too humdrum. We need to ask ourselves about the meaning of life. What is the purpose of life, why should we keep going? The images in our dreams give us that meaning, and at the deepest level they are connected to myths.

Peay: So by asking those questions of ourselves, being continually in the process of questioning life, we are able to connect to life in a more meaningful way?

Woodman: I think so. If we have a dream about a radiant child, we have to ask, "What is the Christ child in me?" Or we may dream about Lucifer or Mary Magdalene. It doesn't matter whether we go to church or a synagogue or a temple—what matters is that we have an archetypal framework which gives our life a universal meaning, so that we are part of humanity, part of some bigger plan. Otherwise we are isolated and alienated.

Peay: What is an archetype?

Woodman: Jung said that just as we are programmed with chromosomes physically, so we are programmed with patterns psychically. These archetypal patterns are like magnets in the unconscious that control what the ego does. These big archetypes—father, mother, divine child—these are the forces underlying our existence. They are energy centers that propel us beyond our transitory existence. You can look back through your life at your relationships and see patterns. Jung said that what you don't bring to consciousness you live out unconsciously. So if you look at your relationships you can begin to see certain patterns. Certainly your dreams will show you archetypes you've been living. I don't think you can do this as a young person. You have to be able to detach enough to look back at your life. By the time you're thirty you should be starting to see a pattern.

Peay: Can you talk about dream work in Jungian analysis?

Woodman: Well, to me it's everything. I rely completely on the guidance of dreams. If a dream is misinterpreted, the dream of the next night will tell you so. As I said earlier, I feel each of us has a destiny to fulfill. If we cooperate with that destiny consciously, and trust the guidance, it's amazing where we go. If we don't follow our destiny, we betray ourselves, the person we could be. We put ourselves in narrow little confines that we have to control because there's chaos outside.

Peay: Is it true, in studying your dreams, that often something comes up that is very different from what one would consciously expect?

Woodman: Yes. We tend to live as far away as possible from our unconscious. Mind you, that's not far, but we do our best to be blind.

Peay: Dream interpretation seems like a lost art, a forgotten language.

Woodman: That's right. Children are better at it than adults, really. Because children are closer to soul. I love English literature, but I know many people say that poetry doesn't make any sense, Shakespeare doesn't make sense! They can't think metaphorically. It's tragic. So to try to interpret dreams, which are pure metaphor, with no help, can be dangerous. But once you get into it, it makes awesome sense. Most images have two sides, you always have to be aware of that double edge.

Peay: It seems odd that these myths that are so ancient have so much to offer the twentieth-century man or woman. You say this is because we have greater distance . . .

Woodman: We have enough distance to allow us to be close.

Peay: To understand it metaphorically, is that what you mean?

Woodman: If you're far enough away from something, you can relate to it at a much more intimate level than something that is just pulsing with intimacy. There's a paradox there.

Peay: I see that paradox. It's as if myth has only just become "myth." The gods and goddesses of ancient Greece weren't considered myths, they were the Greeks' . . .

Woodman: . . . Bible. The soul is eternal. Its language is eternal.

Peay: James Hillman says myth is always the thing you're in and don't know it's a myth. We may have lost certain ancient myths, he says, but we're still living myths. He even says television is a myth.

Woodman: Exactly. Do you see that?

Peay: I think a lot of people might say that if television is a modern myth, it's a pretty paltry example.

Woodman: Well, Aphrodite as an archetype doesn't look much like some of the women on the TV program "Dynasty." Think of the people in the Middle Ages going to church in the cathedral they built with their own hands, and that sense of mystery that pervades the atmosphere . . . the stained glass and the big big church—and *God lives there.* They can go into the presence, and the mystery is bigger than they are. What a difference between that and "Dynasty"!

Peay: Well, it was the author John Updike who said that television has replaced the hearth in the home.

Woodman: I agree with that. People gather around the television—but they don't dream with the flames or watch the mystery in each other's faces, or listen to the mystery in each other's hearts. The mystery's gone. So therefore they look for the mystery in the addiction. I hate to say it again. But what is in the power of a muffin that a woman can get so nervous she can't stand the thought of not having it? She just has to have it, her body shakes and gets hotter and sweats. Got to have the alcohol; got to have sex; got to go and buy some silk underwear. What is the mystery operating there?

Peay: It all seems to come down to the fact that we have no religions that satisfy us spiritually. There's no spirituality in everyday life.

Woodman: Yes. We are human beings. And a human being has a divine, creative intelligence. One way or another that creative intelligence is going to find an outlet. If it can't find an outlet through the imagination, which is its natural route, it will find it in a concretized way. That becomes compulsive because there's no way it can find what it's looking for in a concrete way. You can't find the Divine Mother in gobbling food.

Peay: So when you say this energy can find no way to express itself through the imagination, it's the artistic side, as well as the religious side, of ourselves that we've allowed to atrophy?

Woodman: Which is all tied up in God. We become gods when we create. Matisse said, "I believe in God when I'm working." If our creative energy is blocked, it will find an outlet in some kind of distorted religion, or addiction. An addiction to me is a distorted religion.

Peay: What is the relationship between creativity and religion?

Woodman: Creativity is divine! To me it is the virgin soul opening to spirit and creating the divine child. You cannot live without it. That's the meaning of life, that creative fire.

Peay: So by teaching my son to paint, or encouraging his artistic talents, that is in essence a spiritual act?

Woodman: Exactly. Just give him the paints. Let him go to it and discover his own soul.

13

In Her Own Voice*

So long as a woman accepts a man's archetypal projection,
she is trapped in a male understanding of reality.
—Marion Woodman.

Heavy rain-laden clouds were darkening the afternoon sky, casting an eerie light on the azalea, dogwood and late tulip blossoms. I was sitting at my desk amid scattered notes and books, staring at my writing pad. I was trying to communicate how radically different Jungian analyst Marion Woodman's newest book, *Leaving My Father's House,* is from her previous ones. But after having scratched out several false starts, my pen failed to move. Words that usually could be coaxed out were hiding. I sat empty and puzzled.

Earlier I had stumbled upon a phrase in Woodman's third book, *The Pregnant Virgin.* The quote, from *a New York Times* book review by Carolyn Heilbrun, suggested that language failed women writers who tried to record their experiences because they had been "muted by centuries of training." Woodman had added, "This is no less true of any woman attempting to speak with her own voice." I let the words sink in, but thought, "Well, I'm a writer. I've certainly found thousands, probably millions, of words over the years." But still I sat, frozen.

Gradually it dawned on me that perhaps I was unconsciously used to a masculine mentality and writing style. Could it be that Woodman's new book, the energy behind it and my experience of it were demanding that my writing be more feminine? What constituted feminine writing anyway?

After much thought, I realized that the trouble I was having was due to my approach: I was trying to analyze Woodman's journey through her various books, trying to explain rationally what makes her latest effort so different. I was failing miserably because I was approaching the task through my head. To be true to the book, I had to drop into my belly. I had to balance masculine discrimination—what was relevant to share—with feminine sensibility—what I felt about the book.

---

* Reprinted from *Common Boundary,* vol. 10, no. 4 (July/August 1992). Written by Anne A. Simpkinson, editor of *Common Boundary.*

129

Now I am not keen on first-person journalistic accounts. Most people are not interested in the journalist, they are interested in the story. Personal style and perspective all shape the story being told, but the true art of writing, I believe, is telling the story in your unique voice, with as little ego as possible.

This I believe is precisely what *Leaving My Father's House* is all about. It's about storytelling, about finding and expressing one's feminine voice in such a way that the deeper, more universal, Feminine voice emerges. The stories Woodman so providentially chose are the fairy tale "Allerleirauh," a slice of Woodman's history with the fairy tale, and three women's accounts of their inner journeys as told through journal entries and dream imagery.

Woodman's role was that of a weaver, interlacing interpretative strands of the fairy tale with the women's stories. The unifying thread is their focus on the process of becoming conscious of how we—both women and men—are driven and defined by negative masculine values, how we can heal our feminine nature, and ultimately how we can balance our positive masculine and feminine energies.

Of course, all of Woodman's books deal with these issues. In her first book, *The Owl Was a Baker's Daughter,* she looked at eating disorders, which, she said, were rooted in women's separation from their feminine nature. In her popular *Addiction to Perfection*—over 80,000 copies have been sold since its publication in 1982—Woodman more clearly defines the negative internal voices behind eating disorders and other addictions. Andromeda, the young feminine energy, "terrorized and in danger of being sacrificed to monsters of the unconscious," mentioned in the preface of *Addiction,* is transformed into "the pregnant virgin," the image Woodman used as the title for her third book. There the discussion centers on creativity and the process of soul-making that goes on once the daughter is free of the negative father complex. In *The Ravaged Bridegroom,* Woodman sees the task as raising "the feminine to a new level of consciousness so that matter . . . will be suffused with its own inner light, a radiant container strong enough to relate with vibrancy and creativity to the emerging masculine consciousness."

In *Leaving My Father's House,* her ideas about the patriarchy and the emerging feminine echo these earlier works. But the book presents readers with an entirely different experience. Woodman's previous books seem to offer feminine content in a masculine format. For example, *The Owl Was a Baker's Daughter,* originally her Diploma thesis, reads like the academic paper it was. Charts, references, quotes and case studies lend credibility to her argument but reflect a linear, masculine organization of the material. In later books, Woodman talks about the struggle to find her feminine literary voice. In *Addiction to Perfection,* she says that linear thinking kills her imagination. But still she wrestles with a spiraling writing style and prose densely packed with references, associations and quotes. In her new book, it's as if Woodman integrated her *ideas* about femininity and masculinity with the *form* that contains them. That form consists of two very feminine elements: collaboration and story.

The book actually bears the names of Woodman and the three women—Rita Greer Allen, Mary Hamilton and Kate Danson—who tell their "soul" stories. (Kate Danson, a pseudonym, is used to protect the identity of the woman who talks about being sexually abused by her brother.) Woodman explained how the cooperative venture came to be in a recent interview. She explained that she was "going another round" on the fairy tale "Aller-leirauh" when she saw that these women, who were all working on dream material from the past, were dealing with issues related to the fairy tale.

"I was going deeper into the elements of patriarchy in myself," Woodman recalled, "and I saw how the four stories were beginning to shape into a totality." She also sensed that the stories might be helpful and valuable to others on similar journeys. So she asked each woman if she would be interested in working on her story for publication.

Each agreed and began the arduous task of editing and refining thousands of pages of her own material. The project, which took nearly three years to complete, apparently floundered several times. "Each of us drew back at certain times and said we didn't want to publish," Woodman said. "Yet the dreams of all four of us seemed to say keep with it, do it." The energy that urged the women to continue is alive in the pages of the book. It's one reason why the work is so compelling.

The other reason is because stories are powerful, feminine vehicles of communication. By their very nature, they transport us to the imaginative realm. Stories feed our souls, particularly when told from a deep, inner source of truth. And ultimately this is why *Leaving My Father's House* succeeds. All four women have obviously done intensive work. Their images and metaphors shimmer and resonate in one's imagination. As a reader, I could literally feel images in my psyche being activated. I can attribute at least one dream directly to reading the book, and more than once, while reading it, I got such a strong image in my mind's eye that I had to stop and jot down what I was envisioning before I could continue.

But the proof of the pudding is always in the tasting, so listen now to Marion Woodman, who in an interview tells about her work and new book—in her own voice.

Common Boundary: I want to begin by talking about *Leaving My Father's House*. The book is very different from what you've done in the past. I've found your previous books mentally stimulating but the images in this book resonated in my body. There was also a very interesting weaving of the fairy tale, your interpretation of it and the women's stories.

Marion Woodman: That's what I found interesting, too. The fairy tale's structure holds the stories together as a unit. Each woman had thousands of journal pages that she condensed to between 80 and 100 pages. It was an arduous process because each woman defined the thread of her myth through her dream imagery. Each struggled to free herself from bondage to patriarchal thinking whether in the university, the church, her relationship to her family, even her relationship to her own body. In each story, the unconscious contributed images that not only support, but guide, the process in ways consciousness could never have conceived.

Our culture, as I see it, is evolving toward an ethos in which femininity and masculinity empower each other. The imagery in the dreams of Kate, Mary and Rita shows the psyche moving toward that new integration with a new understanding of the feminine and the masculine, rooted in what I would call *interpenetration.*

In my other books, I always felt handicapped because while I illustrated points with individual dreams, I was aware of how awesome the dream journey is—the psyche elegantly guiding the dreamer who is attentive to healing and wholeness. In this book, we follow particular images for years, so the reader can follow the transformative process.

CB: Certain symbols and images not only recurred within the individual person's journey, but overlapped among the stories. There was a snake and a deer . . .

MW: And a bear, recurrent images in most people's dreams. It's important to point out that there's a huge difference between impersonal and personal imagery in the unconscious process. Some people might say, for example, that I am mother-bashing in this book. But I have said over and over again that I'm talking about the mother complex and the mother archetype. These are influenced by the relationship to the personal mother, but they encompass what we've inherited through 2,500 years in which the feminine has been denigrated. Our mothers were afflicted with a self-image of shame, degradation, self-doubt and low self-esteem; our grandmothers were afflicted too, back through how many generations? Most of us have no idea of the depth of the wounding of the feminine in the unconscious of both men and women. When I write about the tremendous damage that has been done through the negativity of the mother complex, I'm certainly not talking about the personal mother. Our mothers and grandmothers were ravaged in the very cells of their bodies as we are ravaged. Few of them had any way to access their unconscious shame. We have inherited it and are bringing it to consciousness. Jung argued that our actual parents are nominal. Our real parents are our ancestors.

CB: How do you suggest working with this material?

MW: It's very important to be able to recognize the voice of the complex. It's powerful. Ancestral voices are powerful. If you hear a voice deep in your body or in your dreams that says you are no good, that you are a failure, that you don't have any right to live, you may think it's you talking. In fact, it's the voice of the complex. You have to become strong enough to say, "This is the complex talking here. I do not have to submit to it." To stand up and hold your self-esteem while that voice is doing everything it can to pull you down is not easy.

CB: But many people would say, "That voice sounds like my mother."

MW: That's because their mother may have identified with the dark side of the feminine. She may have experienced herself as being judged and, in turn, judged her child. That judgment can paralyze both girls and boys. It can destroy the flow of life. If you are able to distinguish that voice, then you can stand up against it and say, "I choose to live my life." Every addict has to make that choice. "Do I want to follow the unconscious death goddess and die, or do I choose to live my life?" To choose to live is to open to the cherishing side of the mother archetype. That means cutting out the toxins—physical and psychic—that are killing you. It takes immense strength to turn that energy around. Our culture, our planet, is in danger of sinking into the negative mother energy. Redeeming the ancestors is a huge undertaking.

CB: It seems as if there's an incredible internal landscape that we're just becoming familiar with. That inner landscape seems to have its own natural laws.

MW: I think that what you call the inner landscape is a new ethos we are in the midst of shaping. In the early nineteenth century, romanticism constructed an inner landscape that idealized nature. Nature was the nourishing mother. Darwin put an end to that.

Now we are beginning to realize the consequences of ignoring both sides of the mother archetype. We have no time to be sentimental in our thinking or actions. There's a mutation being demanded in the evolution of consciousness. I think that *mater*—the Latin word for mother, the body—wants to become conscious, wants to release light from the density of matter. This is what the French Impressionists were painting. It is where quantum physics and dream imagery meet. This, to me, is the new level of conscious femininity that's never been in the world before: the conscious recognition of energy, wisdom, Sophia, in matter.

That's why my work honors the body as part of the psyche. So often at the psychic level, the process is moving in a very healing direction. But then, I may reach out to touch my analysand and the body pulls back. It doesn't feel worthy. It says, "I am unlovable."

CB: The reaction comes regardless of what they might be consciously thinking or wanting?

MW: Right. As I go deeper into dreams, I realize that the voice that says, "I am unlovable," is in the cells. Therefore it's at that cellular level that the transformation has to take place.

CB: Based on that thinking, do you feel that you're doing psychological work? At one point reading the book, I thought, "This isn't psychology. This is something else." You use the term soul-making. Others might say spiritual development or something of that sort.

MW: Psychological work is soul work. Psychology is the science of the psyche, the soul. Having looked at so many dreams for so many years, I cannot deny that a process guides the soul. By soul, I mean the eternal part of us that lives in this body for a few years, the timeless part of ourselves that wants to create timeless objects like art, painting and architecture. The creative process for me is extremely important. Whenever the ego surrenders to the archetypal images of the unconscious, time meets the timeless. Insofar as those moments are conscious, they are psychological—they belong to the soul. They are in time, illuminating, not rejecting the timeless. They are also in the present. Picasso's "Guernica" is an image of war and chaos; it is also an actual city.

CB: Archetypal psychologists also use the term soul-making. Do you see yourself in that particular branch of Jungian psychology?

MW: No, I don't see myself there. Originally I was a student of English literature. I loved John Keats before I ever heard of psychology. He uses the phrase soul-making. He talks about learning life by heart. Isn't that a wonderful pun? And a sad one.

For me, soul-making is allowing the eternal essence to enter and experience the outer world through all the orifices of the body—seeing, smelling, hearing, tasting, touching—so that the soul grows during its time on Earth. It grows like an embryo in the womb. Soul-making is constantly confronting the paradox that an eternal being is dwelling in a temporal body. That's why it suffers, and learns by heart.

CB: You are talking about a kind of religious experience, aren't you?

MW: Some of us were brought up in a religious faith that we lost in our teens and twenties. But, if we go into analysis, the religious imagery may come back in our dreams, often to our great bewilderment and anger. We thought we were through with that nonsense. But when it comes to us and we dream of a little baby with golden skin and burnished hair, then Christmas becomes something very different.

CB: That reminds me of Rita's story in *Leaving My Father's House.* At the beginning of her section she says that she wants to know God. "I have religious beliefs," she writes. "I just don't know what they are." Then about halfway through her story she remarks, "My search for God is taking me far from the God of my Sunday school. Far from Christianity as I know it, and far from that historical figure called Jesus Christ." But in the end, that's not true at all. Hers is a very poignant journey that comes full circle.

MW: Yes, all three women ran into patriarchal dogma and rejected that dogma and conventional religion because it was dead for them. They saw how patriarchal bureaucracy dominated their experience within the church, so they withdrew from it. But the reality behind the dogma was still in their bones, and it came through in their dreams in totally different ways.

CB: They found the true meaning of the symbol for them.

MW: And the true feeling. I think feeling is crucial. If a symbol isn't resonating in your body, your imagination and your head, it is not working for you. The whole personality—emotion, imagination, intellect—is involved. Jung says you can never really understand the symbol. It is a mystery. Like a diamond, you can see its facets, but you cannot pin it down. You cannot say, "That's exactly what it means," because ten years later it may come again in a dream and your whole body will resonate and you say, "Oh, *that's* what it meant." And, in another ten years, it may come yet again. I'm just beginning to understand dreams I had twenty years ago, and I still don't know what they're fully about.

CB: At certain points the dream feeds you, perhaps to the extent that you can be fed.

MW: Exactly. Symbols are meaningful at the level you're at when you receive them, and that's why they are healing. Metaphor comes out of your bones; it's organic in the body. It resonates and you feel whole. Sometimes you wake up from a dream and you have no idea what the metaphor means, but you feel whole because emotion, imagination and intellect have been brought together, even for a moment. The experience becomes a touchstone because you have experienced wholeness. That's where healing begins.

It's important for us to be in touch with our dreams, because most of us have no models. We don't know what the new feminine is going to be, no idea what the new masculine is. We have to depend on our own imagery to guide us. We have to be able to imagine ourselves moving beyond where we've been before we can even think about going there. It's similar to Olympic jumpers who have to be able to imagine themselves going over the high bar before their physical body can leap with their imaginary body. If they can't imagine it, they can't jump it. They must surrender to energy beyond their conscious effort.

CB: How do you work with the body? Do you work hands-on in sessions or do you tell people to get massages, to dance?

MW: It depends. Sometimes I work in sessions. Sometimes I ask an analysand to go to a specialized body worker. Much of the work goes on in workshops where we work for two hours a week over a period of weeks. Each participant works daily as well as in the workshops because one has to stay with the process and gently go deeper and deeper into what is buried in the muscles: the chronic fear, grief, shame. Suffering opens us to others' grief. Love—a pulsation in the room, a healing power—is released.

We always start with breathing, and spend about a third of the session relaxing. To relax is to allow the breath to go into the depth of the body. When the body is thoroughly relaxed, it can release authentic responses— grief, terror, rage. We are trying to connect with the shadow energies chained in the dungeons of our dreams.

We connect with those energies in many different ways. Through imagery, for example. I use imagery from dreams because I believe that the dream image is the gift of the Self. So we concentrate, put the image into our body and then let it go where it wants to go, change as it wants to change. The transformations are the healing process.

We usually dance, but always with the idea of connecting to the inner core. Nothing is for show, nothing is for fitness. I don't have anything against fitness but if you are connected to the inner core, your body fitness is part of your wholeness.

The other part of our body work involves voice. Women, in particular, have lost their voices. That's true both metaphorically and literally. The voice tends to come from the throat because we're afraid to breathe deeper. We're afraid to hit the pain.

In my workshops, I always work with body and voice specialists who honor dream imagery. We try to release the muscles in the torso, throat and hips in order to allow the voice to come from a natural ground in the body. In this way the participants learn what it is to have a voice that expresses who they are. That takes years because the fear and anger are so great.

The body is what makes us human. Those of us who have been brought up in a patriarchal world tend to stay in our heads. We want to stay with ideals. We want to put spirit ahead of body. We want to live outside the limitations of this poor stupid thing below the neck that can't, or won't, do what we want it to do.

We try to push all the parts of ourselves that we don't like into our bodies: our greed, our jealousy, our lust. All the darkness we don't want to accept, we push down into our muscles, bones and heart. We pretend we have no shadow and try to escape into our heads. Powerful energies are locked in our bodies. Eventually they rebel, usually in illness.

Sometimes people will paint a picture of their body, in terms of color, and there will be black areas where they cannot see any image. Very interesting things often go on around those areas. As soon as the person puts an image there, it starts to transform. Flowers turn into false teeth, which turn into arrows, and the transformation process goes on. The energy starts to move, light comes into that area. I don't think we've begun to touch the power of imagery in the body.

CB: But working with imagery can get a bit ticklish because people may try to impose a particular image on their psyche. They want to be healthy or they want to be more successful, and they use imagery in a willful way, to force reality to change.

MW: That is not the feminine mode. The unconscious has treasures that consciousness has no idea of. If you take your own imagery and allow it to transform as it wants, it will go exactly where it needs to be. In my experience, forcing an image that is not your own does nothing toward healing because you're not surrendering.

Many people, after a heart attack or in the midst of a life-threatening crisis, learn the feminine art of surrendering to a power that they can't intellectually understand. That's what each of those women in the book discovered.

CB: How to surrender to natural processes? Life processes?

MW: What I would call archetypal processes, creative processes in the matrix of the unconscious. The creative matrix is a terrifying abyss because it contains both demons and angels. Some people are overwhelmed by the demons of the past; I guess we all are at some point. But that matrix is where the new seeds are. When life becomes boring and your job is no longer exciting or your marriage is no longer satisfactory, you have to find new life, and that means dropping into that matrix. It often looks like depression. It's black at first because you are in a psychic womb. It's terrifying. Some people can't take it. But every artist knows that's where you've got to go if you're going to find the new light.

CB: Have you experienced that?

MW: Several times. I think it goes in cycles. You move into that new life, and it's tremendously exciting for years. Then all of a sudden it isn't the least bit interesting. I think a lot of people get burned out for this reason. They try to do the thing that was interesting to them twelve years ago. They start running faster and faster, thinking that surely it will be interesting but it's not. They're running like plastic dolls. I've seen dreams where the Great Mother comes in, holds up her hand, and the energy from her hand zaps the doll. The image disintegrates. Then the ego has to find out what the new life is. That can cost you your marriage, it can cost you your job, it can cost you your church. It's terrifying, but it's the only way to grow. Sometimes you have to give all to find all. It sounds simple. T.S. Eliot says it's "A condition of complete simplicity / (Costing not less than everything)."

CB: It's learning to ride energy, learning to trust that energy when in fact everything we've been taught is more solid, more thought out.

MW: A product.

CB: Yes, a product rather than a process.

MW: I don't think it's any more solid merely because most people grab onto it. They think that their security is in their house, their clothes, their job or their money. Suddenly they can't find security in these concrete objects. Where do you look for security if you have no *inner* world? I mean, once you trust the inner world, it is solid because it gives you your authenticity. Once you get used to relying on dreams, for example, it's like having a rudder on a boat—I think of the unconscious here as a sea—dreams will correct the conscious attitude ever so subtly.

CB: If you listen.

MW: If you listen. If you don't, you go off course. People who are used to listening to their inner world feel lost without dreams. They don't know how to function. Sometimes they get too exhausted to remember their dreams. They don't take time in the morning to lie in bed until the dream comes to them, or they're too tired to write it down in the middle of the night. All their energy is going into conscious living and there isn't time to take a walk that will reactivate nature in the body and therefore reactivate the dreams.

CB: Incest is one of the major themes in the fairy tale, "Allerleirauh," and in Kate's story. But, in the concluding chapter, you also talk at great length about psychic incest—what you call "unboundaried bonding"—where the parents, instead of mirroring their child, use the child to mirror themselves. You say that most people don't realize how damaging this psychic incest is.

MW: I have the profoundest sympathy for people who have been physically abused, but increasingly I am seeing the effects of psychic abuse in people who have been "numbed out" by psychic trauma. They cannot take their life in their own hands because a wall cuts them off from their inner world. They've lost the source of their authenticity.

CB: Kate succinctly describes the psychological result of physical abuse when she says, "I could not bear to think that my brother would harm me. Therefore, I thought I must have done something bad to deserve it."

MW: That applies to psychic incest as well. Children get the idea that there's something wrong with them, that they somehow hurt their parents, older brothers, sisters or teachers, and therefore they deserve to be treated as if their own identity did not exist.

That's common in women. If girls are considered second-class citizens, then unconsciously they feel they deserve to be treated that way. Many women treat other women that way. They don't trust them. They take their self-esteem from men; they don't feel self-esteem in being loved by a woman. That's one of the saddest repercussions of patriarchal thinking.

CB: People who have been abused, either sexually abused or physically beaten, sometimes repress the memory. But with psychic incest, it's different because no physical action was taken against them. The hostility or cruelty is all under the surface. Isn't it a little more difficult to identify because of this?

MW: It's more difficult to identify because of our cultural attitudes. As children, we accept the reality in which we are raised as normal. It may have been taken for granted that women serve men, that somehow the feminine is a bit stupid, illogical or naive. If a family member was addicted, everyone pretended it wasn't happening. Everyone kept quiet. If that's how our lives have been structured, there's a terrible tendency to accept that that's what life is. But that's not what life is. We have to keep reminding ourselves that there's another way.

Now we come back to the body. If there's a voice in the cells of your body that says matter—mother, the feminine—is less than spirit—father, the masculine—or if in the family structure, even at an unconscious level, women were considered second to men, those messages are in the cells of the members of that family. People may then dream they're carrying their parents' baggage, wearing their parents' clothes or eye-glasses. They are unconsciously carrying that outworn baggage. They can never pass into a new country with clutter that belongs in the garbage.

CB: Of course, that's different from physical incest, isn't it? Carrying the value system of your parents isn't the same as being violated physically and emotionally?

MW: It's different, but it can still destroy you. If your parents were in a marriage that destroyed them, you will probably go into a marriage like your parents'. You may get caught in the same traps they did if you don't wake up.

What I'm talking about is living your own life. You are an individual soul. You have a right to your own uniqueness, to live your life to the fullest. You can't do that if you are carrying psychic incest wounds. Now, there's no doubt that if there's physical incest, the body is damaged in ways that it is not damaged by psychic incest. But I think that most of us have huge work to do with the despair, terror and rage in our cells encoded through our psychic incest wounds.

CB: You point out in the book that Jung said that we yearn to unite with our mothers and fathers. Without the incest taboo, we would be inclined to stay with mommy or daddy, physically and psychologically. The taboo creates a boundary against that; it forces a separation.

MW: Yes. In that way, the incest taboo is the beginning of consciousness. We cannot go back to our personal mother and father. That's the core of the book: We, as citizens of this planet, are being challenged to find a new relationship to our archetypal parents—God and Goddess. New images, new responses, new energies. We are having to step into adulthood.

That means leaving psychic incest behind.

What delighted me in working on this book was realizing that in leaving the old patriarchal attitudes and conventions behind, a new vitality toward the Mother emerged: love for Her, love for each other and love for the planet. With that energy—love is energy—comes a masculinity that is determined to protect the feminine. That's a new masculine—a very strong, discerning, discriminating light source that empowers the feminine. The two energies work together and make life a birthright.

That's what *Leaving My Father's House* is about: finding an inner core that values life, takes us into life, rather than has us retreat from it. Valuing includes suffering, but suffering opens us to love.

CB: You mention suffering in your book. You said that consciousness demands suffering. What do you mean?

MW: Let's use food addiction as an example. A woman addicted to food knows that her body does not reveal her soul's beauty. The more she tries to escape from the trap (body), the more cruelly she is fettered.

If consciousness comes in, she may think, "I want my soul and body to be one." That means that when her hand is on the refrigerator door, awareness comes in and says, "You're not hungry for what's in the fridge. Take your hand off the refrigerator door. Don't open it! Walk across the room, flick the switch, dance to Chopin. Feel your pain. Live it. Don't try to smother it." That may seem small, but if you're an addict taking your hand off the door feels like death. The wild creature inside you that can't endure pain is not interested in Chopin. To refuse to feed it food releases its rage or despair. To rechannel its energy demands conscious discipline every time the craving for escape threatens to overwhelm the ego.

CB: I guess discipline is a necessary part of the process.

MW: Discipline is a bad word in our culture. People associate it with having to do what they're told. But discipline is quite a lovely word. It comes from the same root as disciple, and it means seeing yourself through the eyes of the teacher who loves you. We have that teacher within ourselves; we also have the wild animal that needs to be disciplined with love. We need all its instinctual energy and wisdom.

CB: That's the bottom line, isn't it?

MW: Yes, letting ourselves express our full spirit without perverting it. Giving it its freedom to be what it is, without using a whip.

CB:: That's a nice image.

MW: Yes. We live with that raw energy boiling underneath. We need to ride it into life instead of toward premature death.

CB: One last question. You had talked about taking a sabbatical. Now that your new book is out, what will you do?

MW: I want to drop back into my own creative matrix for a while. The last year has taken me into depths I need to honor.

There's a point where it's time to just *be:* no deadlines, no scurrying to catch a plane, no revving up for a lecture, just living life as it comes and focusing on the inner journey.

CB: Is this called retirement?

MW: Retirement? Me? I can't imagine retirement. No. The inner world is no less fiery than the outer. I want to immerse myself in that fire—new images, finer tuning. It will be such a relief to have the outer pressure taken off. I'm tired of pressure. It's against the feminine. There's a danger of going into the world and leaving life behind. I want to live each day as it comes. I hate this business of being pinned down two or three years ahead of time. Yes, it's necessary to organize in the outer world, but right now my soul needs to be as free as Blake's butterfly:

> He who binds to himself a joy
> Does the winged life destroy;
> But he who kisses the joy as it flies
> Lives in eternity's sun rise.

14

The Role of the Feminine in the New Era*

Marion Woodman

Though in the Semitic tradition religion is essentially patriarchal—God as father addressing his people by progressively unfolding his will through a line of male prophets that include Moses, Jesus, Muhammad, Bahá'u'lláh—the feminine, while subordinate, nevertheless plays a powerful role. When the Bible speaks of a chosen people, it has in mind a chosen seed, a reference to the impregnating power of the male that refers directly to the Old Testament, to Abraham's testicles as the father of many nations. It is the impregnating male rather than the impregnated female who is given priority. Since, however, the one requires the other, the woman as the vessel of creation receiving into her womb the impregnating seed of the male, the two become one. This union is stressed in the Christian sacrament of marriage in which male and female become one flesh.

At the same time, however, there is in the Book of Genesis the ambivalent figure of Eve as the consort of Adam. Her curious alignment is with the serpent who tempts her to eat of the forbidden fruit, thus initiating what in Christianity is called Original Sin or the Fall of Man. Against this figure of Eve, as if to redeem her from her fallen state, stands in the New Testament the mysterious figure of Mary as the mother of Jesus, who though espoused to Joseph is already pregnant. In the moving accounts of her plight, which placed her in a potentially dangerous relationship to her society—a society that could stone her to death for adultery—she is declared to be a virgin impregnated, not by her husband, but by the Holy Ghost whose divine action is announced by the archangel Gabriel.

While the Qur'án specifically rejects the Christian doctrine of the Incarnation—that Mary is the mother of God—it nevertheless affirms her virginity, describing in more than one of the súrihs the visitation of the archangel Gabriel. If Mary, in the New Testament, is the second Eve, Christ is the second Adam. As Adam and Eve in their relationship enact a fall from Paradise that begins humanity's earthly evolution, so Mary and

* Presented at the International Bahá'í Congress, London, Ontario, 1988. Reprinted from *The Journal of Bahá'í Studies,* vol. 2, no. 1 (1989). Copyright © 1989, Association for Bahá'í Studies. All rights reserved.

her son in their relationship enact a return to it. Hence, especially in the Russian, Greek and Roman Churches, the veneration of the Virgin Mary makes her, as intercessor and redeemer, almost the equal of Christ. It was long believed that like Christ she bodily ascended to heaven, and, in the Papal Bull of 1950, the *Assumptio Maria* [Assumption of Mary] was proclaimed as a dogma of the Church. In this way, through the back door rather than the front, the feminine came to assume in Catholic Christianity a significance almost equal to that of the masculine. The Church as Mother Church bestowed its sacraments through its anointed priesthood, the priests in a particular sense being her sons.

The feminine in Islam has found in Fátimih a form of veneration that is almost as significant as the veneration of Mary in Christianity. Fátimih was the daughter of Muhammad, given in marriage to Muhammad's cousin, 'Alí, named by Muhammad the first Imám, whose function was to initiate believers into the mysteries of the revelations of the prophets, particularly the revelation of Muhammad in the Qur'án. From Fátimih's womb came the second and third Imáms, Imám Hasan and Imám Husayn. She is, therefore, the mother of the Imáms, and especially in Sh'ite Islam, she is venerated as mother of the Imáms. Her womb is sacred, like the womb of Mary, because of what issued from it. Her body is also venerated as a sacred body, the sign of its sacredness being in the veil she wears. Because Islam was essentially a theocracy, no distinction being made between the two kingdoms of earth and heaven, or between the secular and the spiritual in Iran where the majority of the Shí'ahs dwell, the sacred body of Fátimih became identified with the sacred soil of Iran. Her body was described in the mystical sense as the celestial earth.

We cannot begin to understand the Sh'ite revolution under Khomeini or his successors unless we grasp its veneration of Fátimih. The invasion of the materialism of the West epitomized by the United States was viewed by Khomeini and his followers as the tearing aside of Fátimih's veil and the rape of her sacred body. For this reason, the United States is described as the great Satan whose rape of the sacred soil of Iran (a rape that had the permissive sanction of the late Shah) cannot go unpunished. It seems that until Iran is restored to some imagined medieval purity, the revolution will not be complete.

One of the major Shi'ah beliefs concerning Fátimih is that with the reappearance of the Twelfth or Hidden Imám, the Imám Mihdí, Fátimih will appear unveiled as the sign of his return and the day of resurrection. Her unveiling will be as the removing of the seal, identified with Muhammad as the seal of the prophets. With this unveiling, Fátimih will become as the bride at the marriage feast, described by Bahá'u'lláh in one of his Tablets as the unsealing of the wine of reunion.

In 1848 there was held at Badasht a conference of Bábís, over which Bahá'u'lláh presided. The purpose of the conference was to assist the Bábís to wean themselves from Sh'ite Islam so as to establish the Bábí religion as an independent revelation. Attending this conference were the esteemed Táhirih, one of Persia's greatest poets, and the passionate figure Quddús, both of whom were Letters of the Living who would later meet a martyr's death. Each day one of the essential features of the Bábí religion that demonstrated its independence was isolated for particular consideration. On one of these days, the boldest of these features was formally and dramatically pronounced. Táhirih appeared in their midst without her veil, thus boldly announcing the unveiling of Fátimih that proclaimed the emergence of the Hidden Imám.

The shock of seeing Táhirih unveiled was so great that some of the Bábís were unable to accept it and could not embrace the full implications of the revelation of the Báb. In fact, one Bábí, overcome by what he considered Táhirih's blasphemous behavior, slit his throat. Under the protection of Bahá'u'lláh, Táhirih was led from the conference when it finished. Later she was placed under house arrest by the Shi'ahs and finally met her martyrdom, strangled with the silk handkerchief she had carefully saved for this sacred occasion, which she described as her union with her Beloved.

In the martyrdom of Táhirih can be seen emerging in the Bábí religion (and through Bahá'u'lláh into the Bahá'í religion) the significant role that the feminine, despite the strong patriarchal emphasis, has always played in the Semitic tradition. Táhirih stands as much as any woman for the role of the feminine in the new age. She was a Letter of the Living, the only female Letter of the Living, one of Persia's greatest poets in the tradition of Rúmí, and in her bold declaration of the truth of the new day, she chose— perhaps at Bahá'u'lláh's instigation—to declare the new day by affirming without reservation the reality of the feminine.

It is surely not without significance that in Bahá'u'lláh's awakening to his station, as the prophet of the new day, He was addressed by a visionary maid whom He described as the Maid of Heaven who addressed Him as the Most Exalted Pen. While it would be easy to equate this Maid of Heaven with the figure of Fátimih, unveiled to Bahá'u'lláh and through Him to the world—the unsealing of the wine of reunion—it is perhaps equally important to recognize the fact that from time immemorial, inspiration at this level has been identified with a female muse. Milton, for example, in writing the greatest English epic *Paradise Lost,* described a female figure whom he called Urania dictating to him nightly, as he slept, his "unpremeditated verse" (Book 9, 24).

In Jungian psychology, we speak of this inner feminine as the anima, the Latin word for soul. The tragedy and the danger of a patriarchal society is that too often it suffers the terrible consequences of leaving the feminine soul in both men and women in a repressed and abandoned state. Wherever this happens, the ego, unrefined and undeveloped by intercourse with the inner feminine, functions at a brutal, barbaric level, measuring its strength paradoxically by its power to destroy in the name of an inhuman ideal.

The unveiling of Táhirih in Iran in 1848 has its parallels in the unveiling of nuns in present-day Christendom and in the dreams of countless women in the 1980s. One woman, for example, dreamed that she was dressed in her bridal gown ready to meet her bridegroom. Suddenly, she was aware that there was interference, something that she had not taken into account. She was told by a voice in the dream that she must make peace with her sister, a woman who in reality had defied her father by running away to marry but who had suffered a nervous breakdown as a result. A strong feminine voice told the dreamer that she must wear her veil with a Mary Queen of Scots headdress and that her forehead must remain covered or her spiritual eye would be irreparably damaged.

These three themes, the veil, the shadow sister under the power of the old father, and the necessity of protecting the spiritual eye, are characteristic of modern women's dreams and, therefore, one can assume they carry transpersonal as well as personal meaning. Since dreams are contents of the unconscious, which moves ahead of consciousness, such dreams suggest a thrust from the unconscious toward a new way of seeing, but a way that must be integrated at every step. Such dreams make it clear that the woman is not going to the marriage that she anticipated—the union of male and female in one flesh. Nor is she ready for the new marriage because one side of her female self is still in bondage to the old father, still so fragile that although she has the strength to defy her father with his outmoded, rigid concepts of her destiny, she has not the strength to stand to her own truth as Táhirih stood to hers.

Moreover, she must remain sequestered behind her veil, unprepared as yet to step forth, as Táhirih stepped forth with the support of Bahá'u'lláh at the conference of Badasht. That support of Bahá'u'lláh, as the presiding presence, gave her strength. The woman in the dream is warned that her spiritual eye is not yet strong enough to see what it must see before she dare remove the veil. Her spirituality is still too vulnerable to the old dispensation, too vulnerable to the old criticisms and the stones that will be aimed at her when she dares to speak what she knows to be her own truth. One could amplify this dream further with the actual situation that developed between Mary Queen of Scots and her cousin Elizabeth. Torn by intrigues and love affairs with the men around her, Mary put her trust in the Virgin Queen and paid for her naiveté with her life. Although Elizabeth called herself the Virgin Queen, her virginity was born of a masculine consciousness that prided itself in power, not love. Her virginity had nothing to do with the receptivity of feminine consciousness open to the impregnation of the Holy Spirit.

Where a woman has not integrated her own femininity, has not looked into herself for her own inner shadow sister who still values herself according to the laws of the old patriarch (in fairy tales, the old king), she puts herself in a very dangerous position if she takes off her veil too soon. The resultant tragedy is clear in the lives of many nuns who have removed their veils, lost the security of the nunnery walls, and found themselves unable to cope with a sexual, materialistic, brutal world they do not understand, fluctuating between their freedom in the eyes of God and their slavery to their guilt and fear. It is equally clear in the lives of countless women who yearn to throw off the veil of their imprisoning marriage to a father-husband whom they once promised to love, honor and obey, only to realize they have not the inner strength nor the fundamental knowledge of the marketplace to survive, let alone live a free life. They are more afraid of freedom than prison because, although they are seeing with new eyes, they have not the inner marriage which would give them the strength to stand to their own virgin truth—the strength that would allow them to say, "This is who I am." Standing to her truth, Táhirih left her husband.

In another dream, a woman who had been working hard to contact her own inner femininity received a message on a slate, written in the well-formed letters of a conscientious adolescent. She felt she had lost contact with her own inner soul about the age of puberty. The message on her slate read, "I'm not quite with this seeing through the veil nor fashioning it into silk. I love you." The middle-aged dreamer was profoundly moved by the frankness of the message, the honesty that would say, "I don't understand," but quick to add, "I love you," as if to say, "Don't leave me down here in darkness."

In reality the woman had been meditating daily on the meaning of the soul in matter, the energy that can permeate flesh, flower, fish and fowl. Earlier, she had dreamed she met an old woman who gave her oil to rub on her body, and as she rubbed she felt light moving through every molecule of her person until her whole body was one living essence through which she could perceive the essence of the tulip on her desk, the tree outside her window, the song of the cardinal on the branch. This perception stayed with her and made her weep for the ravaging of the planet on which we live. It made her weep too for the ravaging of the human body in our culture, the desecration of the temple of the Holy Spirit.

In the dream of the slate, she felt her own young feminine trying to come to grips with the illusions that blocked her vision of reality. The fashioning into silk, as in Táhirih's use of her silk handkerchief, probably had something to do with the transformation of the sow's ear, the corporeal body into the subtle body, making the corporeal body transparent, translucent, so that one can see through it, beyond it. Or perhaps, from the other side, the young feminine is the soul who perceives from the other side of the veil, neither quite understanding the problems of the body locked in illusions, nor the perception of the body as anything less than finest silk. Perhaps her assurance of love is encouragement to the ego still striving to release itself into the new dispensation.

Release into the new dispensation has nothing to do with profane images of unveiling; it has nothing to do with the so-called freedom of exhibiting the body in a bikini. Not that I have anything against bikinis, but dieting to fit into a bikini is too many women's vision of the unveiling. The unveiling is a spiritual event, the unveiling of the soul that recognizes the sacredness of matter, the sacredness of matter in union with the sacredness of spirit.

Though the comparison of the unveiling of Táhirih to the dreams of modern women may seem to be rather far-fetched, I am making the comparison in an effort not only to honor Táhirih as an example of a renewed feminine consciousness crucial to this new era, but also to stress the universality of the feminine that cuts across all cultural and religious boundaries to affirm in its own way the oneness of humanity.

And now to conclude, perhaps the most beautiful description of the unveiling epitomized by Táhirih is to be found in Shelley's lyrical drama *Prometheus Unbound,* written in 1819 at a time when in Persia the school of Shaykh Ahmad was preparing many Muslims for the coming of the Hidden Imám. In *Prometheus Unbound,* Asia, the feminine soul of Prometheus, has just released him from his bound and limited consciousness to a recognition of himself as the inaugurator of a new age. Asia is addressed by her sister:

> How thou art changed! I dare not look on thee;
> I feel, but see thee not. I scarce endure
> The radiance of thy beauty. Some good change
> Is working in the elements, which suffer
> Thy presence thus unveiled. (2.5.16-20)

The unveiled presence of Asia reminds her sister of Asia's birth as Venus, when, as in Botticelli's painting *The Birth of Venus,* she stood in the veined shell to symbolize the birth of love:

The Nereids tell
That on the day when the clear hyaline
Was cloven at thine uprise, and thou didst stand
Within a veined shell. . . .
. . . .
. . . love, like the atmosphere
Of the sun's fire filling the living world,
Burst from thee, and illumined earth and heaven,
And the deep ocean and the sunless caves,
And all that dwells within them. . . . (2.5.20-30)

It is this bursting of love to fill the living world that is perhaps the best interpretation one can give to the unveiling of Táhirih and to the role of the feminine in the new era. This love is present in matter itself even as the sun's rays are present in the atmosphere. It permeates matter, rendering the earth itself, in Bahá'u'lláh's phrase, "the foot-stool" of God *(Gleanings* 30).

Works Cited

Bahá'u'lláh. *Gleanings from the Writings of Bahá'u'lláh.* Trans. Shoghi Effendi. 2d ed. Wilmette, IL: Bahá'í Publishing Trust, 1976.

Milton, John. *Paradise Lost.* Ed. Scott Elledge. New York: Norton, 1975.

Shelley, Percy Bysshe. *Prometheus Unbound: The Text and the Drafts.* New Haven, CT: Yale University Press, 1968.

15

Human Potential Through Dance*

Marion Woodman

When I was asked to speak at this Congress, I felt genuine excitement. Someone had recognized my secret passion. Every day I dance in my living room—my joy, my anguish, my thanksgiving. I am sure I will be a dancer in heaven. Being recognized on Earth was like flying free from a cage. When I began to prepare my talk, however, my wings were clipped.

"Why is a Jungian analyst speaking to dancers?" I asked myself.

Some of you may be asking the same question.

Well, I have found an answer. What lies at the center of your work and mine is imagery. Images are the bridge between consciousness and the unconscious. Any powerful image is energized by a precarious balance of tensions that intersect at a point that is both in time and timeless. In sleep, we dream. Our instinctual nature produces images that reveal our spiritual condition. We may be running as fast as we can, but in spite of immense exertion we are running in slow motion on the spot. An accurate image of our hurly-burly lives! Think of Tatiana in Kranko's *Onegin*. She is a woman caught between her conscious responsibility as dutiful wife to her husband and her deeper responsibility to herself as a passionate woman still in love with a man who rejected her.

Samuel Beckett is a master of creating the dance of life on the stage with the simplest dialogue. His unforgettable images cut through to the starkest truths. In *Endgame*, for example, blind Hamm reigns over his eight-foot square kingdom from his wheelchair, sardonically ridiculing his old parents whom he imprisons in garbage cans beside him, at the same time tyrannizing his servant Clov, on whom he is dependent. Clov, with his suitcase packed, stands at the beginning of the play, and at the end, paralyzed in the doorway, trying to leave, unable to go. The starkness of the visual image resonates through body, mind and heart as we sense ourselves poised on a pinhead between the transitory and the eternal worlds. As T.S. Eliot writes in *Four Quartets:*

> Except for the point, the still point,
> There would be no dance, and there is only the dance.

---

* Address to Dance Congress (CORD), Toronto, July 1988.

The still point between the two worlds is the hallmark of great art, as it is the hallmark of a life being truly lived.

Unforgettable images seem simple because they are true to individual, personal experience. They are not simple, however, because they evoke the deepest conflicts of life and death common to us all. They resonate in our depths because they activate the primordial energies present in our unconscious. These energies Jung called archetypes. He believed that

> their origin can only be explained by assuming them to be deposits of the constantly repeated experiences of humanity. . . . The images contain not only all the fine and good things that humanity has ever thought and felt, but the worst infamies and devilries of which men have been capable. Owing to their specific energy—for they behave like highly charged autonomous centres of power—they exert a fascinating and possessive influence upon the conscious mind and can produce extensive alterations in the subject.**

Let me illustrate. If I put this piece of paper over a magnet, you cannot see the magnet. But if I throw iron filings on top of the paper, they will take a shape determined by the unseen magnet. Metaphorically, the filings are the *personal* associations and memories that are drawn to the energy field of the magnetic archetype, the *universal* bond. We cannot see the archetype, but we can see the archetypal image. The eternal world is revealed through personal images. The timeless through time. Thus when Macbeth hears that what was left of his feminine soul is dead, he cries, "Out, out brief candle"—and our own soul quakes at the prospect of going out into the ultimate darkness.

While the image carries personal associations, the archetype is charged with transpersonal energy. We all have our own personal image of mother, but at the core of that image is the universal goddess in her positive and negative aspects. Positively, she is the nourisher, the caregiver, the creative matrix; negatively, she is the destroyer, the evil witch that sucks the life out of her children and turns them to stone.

Archetypal energies appear in different guises in ancient and modern cultures around the world. As cultures evolve the images change, but the magnetic energy does not change. Shiva and Shakti in divine union, for example, is an image that still propels us in our search for the perfect mate. In someone who is unconscious, the yearning for that ideal can so overwhelm the ego that the person is driven from bed to bed in search of the eternal perfection. Iphigenia, sacrificed by her father Agamemnon in the ancient Greek story, can take hold of an unconscious teen-ager who

---

** *Two Essays on Analytical Psychology,* CW 7, pars. 109-110.

adores her father-teacher, and she will sacrifice herself in every possible distortion of her femininity to please him. Gelsey Kirkland almost lost her life in her adoration of Balanchine; her book is entitled *Dancing on My Grave.* Nijinsky opened himself to the archetypal energies that electrified his dance and resonated in the very souls and viscera of his audience, but his ego was not strong enough and he succumbed to madness.

Individuals and cultures either relate to their inner gods and goddesses consciously, or they are possessed by them unconsciously. So long as consciousness is strong enough and disciplined enough to open itself to that archetypal energy, enter into that eternal world and return again to its humanity, it thrives. If, on the other hand, consciousness cuts itself off from that world so that the dialogue of the opposites ceases, then the archetypal images become lifeless stereotypes, old-fashioned empty containers. Then the archetypal energies manifest in perverted, addictive behavior. When the energy of the archetype ceases to ignite consciousness, both the culture and the individual lives created around it disintegrate.

Dance is archetypal imagery. Without words, without clay, without paint, the body becomes the image. Prehistoric cultures painted their dances on the walls of caves. Australian Aborigines dance their hunts and battles, hoping to attract divine attention. Navajos and Hopis dance their dance for rain, and many of us in the past drought-stricken weeks have either danced our dance or understood in our bones what that dance is about. The steady beat activates the central nervous system that in turn releases the healing power of the instinctual unconscious, often accompanied by a healing image or voice.

In professional dance, we can see how the numinous fires of one century became dead wood in the next. The great male dancers of the seventeenth and eighteenth centuries, Gaetano Vestris and his son Auguste among them, were famous for their elegance, power, nobility and presence. Then came the French and American Revolutions and Romanticism. Different archetypes were constellated. Aided by the strengthened toe-shoe, female dancers became light, dainty dolls supported by their stodgy male partners. Russia held to the image of male virility, and when Serge Diaghilev and the Ballets Russes arrived in Paris, Pavlova and Nijinsky were among that powerful troupe.

Then archetypal energies shifted, tearing great holes in the diaphanous veils of Romanticism. In 1961, Rudolf Nureyev left the Kirov Ballet in Paris and electrified the Western world with his presence both on and off the stage. The regenerated masculine archetype was given another blood transfusion when in 1971 Baryshnikov arrived in the West. Since then, audiences no longer think of dance as a disembodied world of wan ballerinas partnered by effeminate males. Nor is current Western culture interested in such an image.

This brief historical sketch may help to clarify the power of an archetypal image in a culture. Romanticism was a major upheaval of unconscious, irrational energies that destroyed the controlled eighteenth-century Age of Reason. *Swan Lake* images the misty, murky dangerous world of the unconscious in which the male becomes aware of his soul guide, sometimes as Odile—the idealized, ethereal feminine without substance—and sometimes as Odette—the vicious seductress ready to lure him out of life. *Swan Lake* is still popular because that split in femininity is still present in men and still unresolved in many women. In art, as in life, matter gives substance to soul. The images are the metaphors that make our own spiritual condition evident before our very eyes. If they are merely beautiful forms disconnected from the instincts, they are lifeless decorations, affectations, boring stereotypes.

Without a direct line to the archetypal level, people sooner or later become depressed. Life becomes two-dimensional, a daily round of treadmill existence. Creativity dries up because daily communication with the creative matrix is gone. Ideas are no longer exciting. The style that was once the right container is dull. Archetypes have become stereotypes. The resulting depression, if it is not masked by pills or addictive behavior, takes them into the death of the old to make room for the birth of the new. It is a painful but natural part of every person's journey to wholeness. Moreover, artists, whose energy is more concentrated in the unconscious than in consciousness, are the voices of the future. They are in close touch with the revolutionary thrust of the unconscious that will eventually overthrow the conscious standpoint. That pioneer country can be terrifying. It can feel like insanity. The line between genius and madness is not a strong wall.

The connection between conscious and unconscious poses particular problems in the dancer because the body is the soul in action. A poet, T.S. Eliot, for example, can recognize himself producing "a heap of broken images." He can remain invisible while he sends his heap off to a friend, Ezra Pound, to scrutinize and put into a form that becomes the revolutionary *Waste Land.* The body, however, makes the soul visible and soul conflicts become body conflicts that are obvious to everyone watching. In my analytic work, for instance, a patient can be saying one thing while the body is saying the opposite. By stopping the blather and allowing the body to express itself, the abandoned soul can reveal its repressed anger and anguish. From my work with dancers, I know the intensity of the struggle that exists between devotion to aesthetic form and the ways of nature. A sylph-like body may be an exquisite container, but if it is achieved through prolonged starvation, the connections to the archetypal depths are eventually lost because the instincts are being betrayed. Loving discipline is one thing; whipping an animal into submission is another.

The problem of the deadly perfect is a killer not only in dance but in our culture too. Addiction to perfection leads to the compulsive drive to control more, possess more, excel more. The "more, more, more" focus in one specialized direction is not natural to life. Certainly in the artistic world it achieves exactly what many artists want: an escape from life. They hate ugliness, war, absurdity, chaos, loss of control. Like Hamm, they want to be God in their eight-by-eight kingdom. And so they put all of their energy into honing life into a rigid, tiny experience, telling the same story over and over again to ashen stereotypes. Like Hamm, they end up blind and crippled, and like Clov, paralyzed, trying to leave and unable to go. What they fail to take into account is that they are human beings who live like everything else according to basic laws of balance.

If we find ourselves dancing, however beautifully, around a hole at the center, we have to recognize that that hole is volcanic. The energies of the rejected instincts will eventually erupt and notify us in no uncertain terms that we are human beings. The eruption may take the form of an addiction to starvation, drugs, sex, or whatever. It may break out in illness. It may suddenly be a body that roars, "I will not be whipped any longer. I will not be starved. I will not be driven when I am exhausted. I have a wisdom of my own and I will try to save my bodysoul."

Women dancers in particular are at a real turning point in relationship to their bodies. If they find their self-esteem in the approval of men, they need to realize that what most men are projecting onto them is their own disembodied soul or their own Earth Mother. Neither projection recognizes the mature, embodied woman who has the courage to be who she is. And being who she is involves loving her body, nourishing her, honoring her needs, celebrating her as the temple for her soul. This poses particular conflict for the dancer because her body is her artistic instrument, and as an image for a modern audience it must be anorexically thin. Women need to think about this image. Are we unconsciously colluding with men's soul images, souls that don't want to be here, souls without substance that yearn to fly in ethereal abandon? What is the right container for a mature woman who lives in her body?

The dancer develops the body with infinite patience and hard physical discipline, in order to create a container that is strong enough and flexible enough to receive the penetration of the divine energy from the unconscious. Archetypally, feminine matter opens itself to masculine spirit. However well disciplined the muscles are, however perfect the technique, without the spontaneous opening to transcendent power, the dance lacks life. The form is not filled with spirit.

My own memories of Margot Fonteyn illustrate this point. In 1952, I saw her in what was to have been her final performance. Her movement was exquisite, her technique flawless. But she was not in the movement, not in a deep soul connection that would allow her body to transmit archetypal light. She was a magnificent diamond, brilliant but cold.

In 1961, the young Tatar, Nureyev, arrived and a new Fonteyn was born. He constellated her innermost soul connection and the woman and the dancer became one, not only with herself, but with him and the audience. I was in Covent Garden the first night they danced *Marguerite and Armand,* the ballet created by Fredrick Ashton for Nureyev. Both of them were totally concentrated. Then a hush fell over the audience. The two bodies danced as one body. Some presence came through them that filled the audience with what I can only describe as a mystical experience of God. When it was over, there was a long silence. They were as still as we. Then the audience burst into tears, into applause, into the aisles, into the foyer to gather daffodils from the jardinieres to throw onto the stage. For twenty minutes, Covent Garden was a yellow waterfall, with daffodils splashing from the box seats and the galleries. Fonteyn was a luminous pearl and Nureyev every inch a man, part animal, part divine. New life was born that night. The stereotype that had been so deadly perfect was filled with new and vital energy. Perhaps the archetype of the androgyne breathed its first breath in a new era.

Indeed, the androgyne may be the archetype that is struggling to emerge in our culture. Androgyny is not unisex, where male and female lose their boundaries and mush together. Magnetic poles must be differentiated if they are to attract each other. What is differentiated masculinity? What is differentiated femininity? How do those two energies interact and balance each other? What is conscious matter? How can we build it into a container strong enough to endure the penetration of energies so immense that we have no idea what they are?

Our planet is now so overbalanced on its way to disembodied spirit that nature is beginning to take its revenge. Like addicts, we blindly go on denying that we are hurtling toward our own annihilation. In our gluttonous fear, we poison our atmosphere, we cut down our rain forests, we allow our magnificent animals to become extinct.

Dancers, you are the priests and priestesses of the bodysoul. Your bodies speak the universal language that can be understood by all the citizens of our planet. The time for ethereal stereotypes is past. What is the *archetype* that will save our Earth?

Index

156

Studies in Jungian Psychology by Jungian Analysts

Sewn Paperbacks

By Marion Woodman:

The Owl Was a Baker's Daughter: Obesity, Anorexia Nervosa and the Repressed Feminine. ISBN 0-919123-03-1. Illustrated. 144 pp. $16

Addiction to Perfection: The Still Unravished Bride
ISBN 0-919123-11-2. Illustrated. 208 pp. $18pb/$20hc

The Pregnant Virgin: A Process of Psychological Transformation
ISBN 0-919123-20-1. Illustrated. 208 pp. $18pb/$20hc

The Ravaged Bridegroom: Masculinity in Women
ISBN 0-919123-42-2. 224 pp. $18

New, Recent and Choice:

The Middle Passage: From Misery to Meaning in Midlife
James Hollis ISBN 0-919123-60-0. 128 pp. $15

Close Relationships: Family, Friendship, Marriage
Eleanor Bertine ISBN 0-919123-46-5. 160 pp. $16

Eros and Pathos: Shades of Love and Suffering
Aldo Carotenuto ISBN 0-919123-39-2. 144 pp. $16

Descent to the Goddess: A Way of Initiation for Women
Sylvia Brinton Perera ISBN 0-919123-05-8. 112 pp. $15

The Creation of Consciousness: Jung's Myth for Modern Man
Edward F. Edinger ISBN 0-919123-13-9. Illustrated. 128 pp. $15

The Illness That We Are: A Jungian Critique of Christianity
John P. Dourley ISBN 0-919123-16-3. 128 pp. $15

Jungian Dream Interpretation: A Handbook of Theory and Practice
James A. Hall, M.D. ISBN 0-919123-12-0. 128 pp. $15

Phallos: Sacred Image of the Masculine
Eugene Monick ISBN 0-919123-26-0. 30 illustrations. 144 pp. $16

Personality Types: Jung's Model of Typology
Daryl Sharp ISBN 0-919123-30-9. Diagrams. 128 pp. $15

The Sacred Prostitute: Eternal Aspect of the Feminine
Nancy Qualls-Corbett ISBN 0-919123-31-7. Illustrated. 176 pp. $18

The Cassandra Complex: Living with Disbelief
Laurie Layton Schapira ISBN 0-919123-35-X. Illustrated. 160 pp. $16

Liberating the Heart: Spirituality and Jungian Psychology
Lawrence W. Jaffe ISBN 0-919123-43-0. 176 pp. $18

Getting To Know You: The Inside Out of Relationship
Daryl Sharp ISBN 0-919123-56-2. 128 pp. $15

*Prices and payment (check or money order) in $U.S. (in Canada, $Cdn)
Add Postage/Handling: 1-2 books, $2; 3-4 books, $4; 5-8 books, $7*

Write or phone for complete Catalogue

INNER CITY BOOKS, Box 1271, Station Q
Toronto, ON, Canada M4T 2P4   **Tel. (416) 927-0355**